GCSE OCR 21st Century
Additional Science
The Workbook

This book is for anyone doing **GCSE OCR 21st Century Additional Science** at higher level.
It covers everything you'll need for your year 11 exams.

It's full of **tricky questions**... each one designed to make you **sweat** — because that's the only way you'll get any **better**.

There are questions to see **what facts** you know. There are questions to see how well you can **apply those facts**. And there are questions to see what you know about **how science works**.

It's also got some daft bits in to try and make the whole experience at least vaguely entertaining for you.

What CGP is all about

Our sole aim here at CGP is to produce the highest quality books — carefully written, immaculately presented and dangerously close to being funny.

Then we work our socks off to get them out to you — at the cheapest possible prices.

Contents

MODULE C6 — CHEMICAL SYNTHESIS

MODULE P4 — EXPLAINING MOTION

MODULE P5 — ELECTRIC CIRCUITS

MODULE P6 — RADIOACTIVE MATERIALS

Published by CGP

Editors:
Joe Brazier, Emma Elder, Mary Falkner, Murray Hamilton, David Hickinson, Helen Ronan,
Lyn Setchell, Hayley Thompson, Jane Towle, Dawn Wright.

Contributors:
Mike Dagless, Jane Davies, Paddy Gannon, Dr Giles R Greenway, Dr Iona M J Hamilton,
Frederick Langridge, Sidney Stringer Community School, Paul Warren.

ISBN: 978 1 84762 751 3

With thanks to Charlotte Burrows, Ben Fletcher, Ian Francis, Julie Jackson, Jamie Sinclair
and Sarah Williams for the proofreading.

With thanks to Jan Greenway, Laura Jakubowski and Laura Stoney for the copyright research.

Page 46 contains public sector information published by the Health and Safety Executive
and licensed under the Open Government Licence v1.0.

Data on page 121 courtesy of NPL http://www.npl.co.uk © Crown copyright 2006.

Printed by Elanders Ltd, Newcastle upon Tyne.
Clipart from Corel®
Based on the classic CGP style created by Richard Parsons.

Cell Structure and Function

Q1   Draw lines to match the **enzymes** for different reactions to where they're found in a **plant cell**.

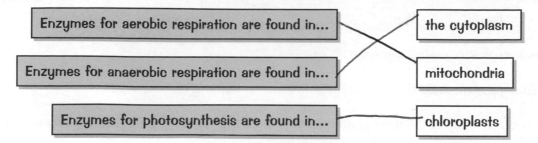

Enzymes for aerobic respiration are found in...   the cytoplasm

Enzymes for anaerobic respiration are found in...   mitochondria

Enzymes for photosynthesis are found in...   chloroplasts

Q2   Complete each statement below by circling the correct word(s) from each pair.

a)   The reactions of **anaerobic /(aerobic)** respiration occur in the **(mitochondria)/ chloroplasts**.

b)   The **(cell membrane)/ nucleus** allows water and gases to pass freely in and out of a cell.

c)   **(Proteins)/ DNA** molecules are made in the **chloroplasts /(cytoplasm)**.

Q3   Fill in the blanks in the passage using the words provided below.
Some words can be used more than once.

proteins	nucleus	chlorophyll	enzymes

DNA is found in the ....Nucleus............... . It contains the instructions for making

........proteins............, for example the ....enzymes........ involved in photosynthesis,

which are found in chloroplasts along with ......chlorophyll............ .

Q4   Place a tick in the table to show the different parts that are
found in each cell type. Some have been done for you.

	Animal cell	Yeast cell	Bacterial cell
Nucleus	✔		
Cytoplasm			✔
Cell membrane			
Cell wall		✔	
Mitochondria			
Circular DNA molecule			

Top Tips: If there's one thing you need to know inside out and back to front it's cells,
because all the other stuff that crops up in Module B4 involves them in some way. When it comes
to life's fundamental processes, cells are pretty much the hippest place to be. Really.

Enzymes

Q1 a) Write a definition of the word '**enzyme**'.

Proteins that speed up chemical reactions

b) Complete the following sentence:

Enzymes are made from *instructions* that are carried in genes.

c) What is the name of the area of an enzyme where the substrate joins and the reaction occurs?

Active site

d) In the box below, draw a series of labelled sketches to show the **lock and key model**.

Q2 This graph shows the results from an investigation into the effect of **temperature** on the rate of an **enzyme-controlled** reaction.

a) What is the **optimum** temperature for this enzyme?

35° C

b) Tick the box next to the statement which correctly describes the results shown in the graph.

The rate of reaction increased until the enzyme was used up. ☐

The rate of reaction increased with increasing temperature up to the enzyme's optimum temperature. ☑

c) Explain what happens to the enzyme at **45 °C**.

It denatures, the hot temperature cause

I'm melting, melting. What a world, what a cruel, cruel world.

Module B4 — The Processes of Life

Enzymes

Q3 Stuart has a sample of an enzyme and he is trying to find out what its **optimum pH** is. Stuart tests the enzyme by **timing** how long it takes to break down a substance at different pHs. The results of Stuart's experiment are shown below.

pH	time taken for reaction in seconds
2	101
4	83
6	17
8	76
10	99
12	102

a) Draw a line graph of the results on the grid below.

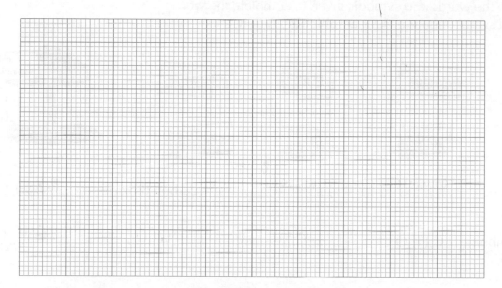

b) Roughly what is the **optimum pH** for the enzyme?

....

c) Explain why the reaction is very slow at certain pHs.

....

....

d) Would you expect to find this enzyme in the **stomach**? Explain your answer.

....

....

The stomach has a low pH.

Top Tips: Enzymes crop up all the time in Biology so it's worth spending plenty of time making sure you know all the basics. This stuff is also dead useful if you end up sitting next to someone with Desirability for a middle name at a dinner party — nobody can resist a bit of optimum pH chat.

4

Aerobic Respiration

Q1 Tick the correct boxes to show whether the sentences are **true** or **false**.

		True	False
a)	Respiration is a series of chemical reactions that release energy.	✓	☐
b)	Large food molecules are made by respiration.	☐	✓
c)	Aerobic respiration releases more energy than anaerobic respiration.	✓	☐
d)	Aerobic respiration requires oxygen.	✓	☐
e)	Breathing is a kind of respiration.	✓	☐
f)	Microorganisms do not respire aerobically.	☐	✓

Q2 Use the words and symbols given to complete the word and symbol equations for **aerobic respiration**.

oxygen   6CO$_2$ 6H$_2$O

water   6O$_2$ glucose

I told you aerobic respiration made energy.

Do you think anyone will notice I blew up the house?

word: Glucose + ~~water~~ Oxygen → carbon dioxide + water ~~oxygen~~ (+ energy)

symbol: $C_6H_{12}O_6$ + 6O$_2$ → 6CO$_2$ + 6H$_2$O (+ energy)

Q3 The **energy** released by **respiration** is used to make **large molecules** (polymers) from smaller ones.

a) Describe how two different polymers are synthesised using the energy released by respiration.

1. Glucose - ~~amino~~ Glucose ~~acid~~ join with Nitrate molecules to mane proteins used in Protein Synteess.

2. Amino Acids joined together to make proteins.

b) Give two other processes that use the energy released by respiration.

1. Photosynthesis

2.

Anaerobic Respiration

Q1   Complete the following sentences by circling the correct word(s).

a)   Anaerobic respiration takes place in animal and plant cells and
some microorganisms when there is **lots of** / **little or no** oxygen.

b)   Plant roots respire anaerobically in **dry** / **waterlogged** soil.

c)   Only bacteria that respire anaerobically can survive **under** / **on top** of your skin.

d)   During **vigorous** / **gentle** exercise your muscle cells respire anaerobically
because the body can't get enough oxygen to them fast enough.

Q2   Anaerobic respiration produces different **products** in different cells.

a)   Use the words given below to complete the **word equations** for anaerobic respiration below.
You may need to use some of the words more than once.

carbon dioxide	ethanol	energy	glucose

   i) Plant cells: **glucose** → .... + ... (+ ....)

   ii) Animal cells: .... → **lactic acid** (+ ....)

b)   Name the two **chemicals** that are produced by anaerobic respiration in **yeast**:

   1. ....

   2. ....

Q3   **Fermentation** is when microorganisms break down sugars
into other products by respiring anaerobically. Describe how
fermentation is used to produce the following:

a)   Biogas

   ....

   ....

   ....

b)   Bread

   ....

   ....

c)   Alcohol

   ....

6

Photosynthesis

Q1   **Photosynthesis** takes place in plant cells and in some microorganisms.

   a)   What is photosynthesis?

   ....

   b)   Use some of the words below to complete the word equation for photosynthesis.

   carbon dioxide   nitrogen   water   glucose   sodium chloride

   light energy

   .... + ... ➜ .... + **oxygen**

   c)   Use some of the symbols below to complete the symbol equation for photosynthesis.

   $6O_2$ $6N_2$ $6H_2O$ $C_6H_{12}O_6$ $6NaCl$

   light energy

   $6CO_2$ + ... ➜ .... + ...

   d)   Draw lines to match each word below to its correct description.

   chlorophyll   a green substance needed for photosynthesis

   oxygen   the food that is produced by photosynthesis

   sunlight   a waste product of photosynthesis

   glucose   supplies the energy for photosynthesis

Q2   Plants use the **glucose** produced by photosynthesis for many things.
   Complete the following passage using some of the words provided.

   cellulose   nitrogen   soil   energy   chlorophyll   starch

   Plants use glucose in respiration to release .... Plants convert

   glucose into .... for storage. Glucose is also converted into

   substances like .... and .... It can also be

   combined with .... from nitrates taken up from the

   .... and used to make amino acids.

Q3   Explain why organisms that photosynthesise form the start of **food chains**.

   ....

   ....

Rate of Photosynthesis

Q1   State what a **limiting factor** of photosynthesis is.

....

Q2   Seth investigated the effect of different concentrations of **carbon dioxide** on the rate of photosynthesis of his Swiss cheese plant. He measured the rate of photosynthesis with increasing light intensity at **three** different CO_2 concentrations. The results are shown on the graph below.

a) What effect does increasing the concentration of CO_2 have on the rate of photosynthesis? Use the graph and your own knowledge.

0.1% CO₂
0.07% CO₂
0.04% CO₂

....

....

....

b) Explain why all the lines level off eventually.

....

Think about a third limiting factor.

....

Q3   Lucy investigated the **volume of oxygen** produced by pondweed at **different intensities of light**. Her results are shown in the table below.

Relative light intensity	1	2	3	4	5
Volume of oxygen produced in 10 minutes (ml)	12	25	37	48	61

bubbles of oxygen
pondweed

a) Plot a graph of her results.

b) Describe the relationship shown on the graph between light intensity and photosynthesis rate.

....

....

....

c) Would you expect this relationship to continue if Lucy continued to increase the light intensity? Explain your answer.

....

....

Rate of Photosynthesis

Q4 The rate of photosynthesis in some pondweed was recorded by counting the number of bubbles of oxygen produced per minute at equal intervals during the day.

No. bubbles per minute	Time of day
10	06.00
20	12.00
10	18.00
0	

a) The time for the final reading is missing. Predict what the time is likely to be.

....

b) Explain why the rate of photosynthesis is 0 bubbles per minute for this time of day.

....

....

c) Plot a **bar graph** on the grid on the right to display the results shown in the table.

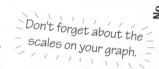
Don't forget about the scales on your graph.

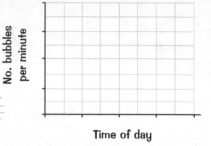
No. bubbles per minute

Time of day

Q5 The table shows the average daytime summer **temperatures** in different habitats around the world.

Habitat	Temperature (°C)
Forest	19
Arctic	0
Desert	32
Grassland	22
Rainforest	27

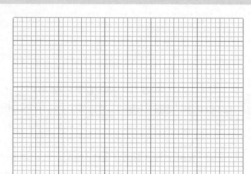

a) Plot a **bar chart** for these results on the grid.

b) From the temperatures, in which area would you expect the smallest number of plants to grow?

....

c) Suggest a reason for your answer above using the terms **enzymes** and **photosynthesis**.

....

....

Q6 Farmer Fred doesn't put his cows out during the winter because the grass is **not growing**.

a) Give **one** difference between summer and winter conditions that affects the rate of photosynthesis.

....

b) How are the rate of photosynthesis and the growth rate of the grass related?

....

....

Module B4 — The Processes of Life

Investigating Photosynthesis

Q1   Sandy is investigating the effect of **light** on the distribution of a plant species. She's thinking about the things she could use to help her collect data.

a)   Name a piece of equipment Sandy could use to measure the level of light.

....

b)   Sandy decides to use a **quadrat** in her investigation.

    i)   What is a quadrat?

    ....

    ii)   Describe how a quadrat can be used to estimate the **percentage cover** of a plant species.

    ....

    ....

c)   In her investigation Sandy uses a **transect**.

    i)   What are transects used for?

    ....

    ii)   Put the following stages in the correct order to describe how to take a transect by writing numbers in the boxes next to them.

       ☐   Start at one end of the tape measure and collect your data.

       ☐   Keep moving along the tape measure and collecting your data until the other end is reached.

       ☐   Run a tape measure between two fixed points.

       ☐   Move along the tape measure and collect your data again.

d)   Sandy carries out her investigation and she finds a type of plant that she doesn't recognise. Use the key to **identify** the plant from the sample shown below.

1.	Does the plant have seeds?	Yes – go to 2.
		No – go to 3.
2.	Does the plant have flowers?	Yes – it is a flowering plant.
		No – it is a conifer.
3.	Does the plant have long stems	Yes – it is a fern.
	with lots of small leaves?	No – it is a moss.

Type of plant: ....

Diffusion, Osmosis and Active Transport

Q1   Complete the passage below by circling the correct word in each pair.

> Diffusion is the **active / passive** overall movement of molecules from a region of
>
> their **higher / lower** concentration to a region of their **higher / lower** concentration.
>
> For example, the movement of **carbon dioxide and oxygen / water and salts**
>
> in and out of plant leaves happens by diffusion.

Q2   Look at the diagram and answer the questions below.

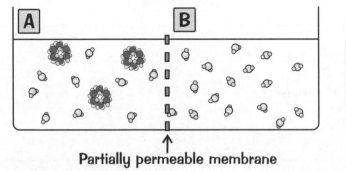

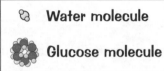

Water molecule

Glucose molecule

Partially permeable membrane

a)   On which side of the membrane is there the **highest** concentration of water molecules?

....

b)   Predict whether the level of liquid on side **B** will **rise** or **fall** over time. Explain your answer.

The liquid level on side B will ...., because ....

....

Q3   **Active transport** is an important process that takes place in living organisms.

a)   Define active transport.

....

....

b)   Give an example of active transport in plants.

....

Top Tips: Osmosis, active transport and diffusion are some of the ways that things can move
in and out of your cells. Osmosis and diffusion just simply happen without any help, whereas active
transport needs a helping hand — it needs energy to get stuff moving.

Module B4 — The Processes of Life

Mixed Questions — Module B4

Q1   Circle the correct word equation for **aerobic respiration**.

glucose + oxygen → carbon dioxide + water (+ energy)

protein + oxygen → carbon dioxide + water (+ energy)

glucose + carbon dioxide → oxygen + water (+ energy)

Q2   **Diffusion** and **osmosis** are ways that molecules move into and out of cells.

a)   Connect the term with the correct definition by drawing a line.

| Diffusion |
| the overall movement of water from a dilute to a more concentrated solution through a partially permeable membrane. |

| Osmosis |
| the passive overall movement of particles from a region of their higher concentration to region of their lower concentration |

diffusion is an essential life process

b)   Give **one** example of osmosis in plants.

....

Q3   Plants use photosynthesis to produce **glucose**.

a)   **i)** Name the other **product** of photosynthesis

....

ii) Name the two **reactants** of photosynthesis.

1. ....

2. ....

b)   List three things that plants use glucose for.

1. ....

2. ....

3. ....

c)   Give **one** example of another organism that uses photosynthesis to produce glucose.

....

Module B4 — The Processes of Life

Mixed Questions — Module B4

Q4 Graham is growing flowers in his greenhouse. Their **rate** of **photosynthesis**, and so rate of growth, **slows** during the **winter**.

Photo-Synthesis Studios
Specialists in photos of:
• families on sheepskin rugs.
• people in poses they'd never normally strike.
• wannabe models.

Special offer Buy one frame, get one free.

a) Circle **two** factors below that limit the rate of photosynthesis.

length of a plant's roots   amount of soil

amount of light   amount of carbon dioxide

b) Name **one** other factor that can limit the rate of photosynthesis.

....

c) Graham wants to speed up the rate of growth of his flowers.
What could Graham add to his greenhouse in the **winter** for better growth?

....

Q5 **Enzymes** are involved in lots of chemical reactions.

a) Tick the correct boxes to show whether the sentences are **true** or **false**.

True False

i) Most enzymes are made of fat. ☐ ☐

ii) Enzymes need a specific constant temperature to work at their optimum. ☐ ☐

iii) The active site is where the substrate joins onto the enzyme. ☐ ☐

iv) A denatured enzyme is an enzyme that's been artificially manufactured. ☐ ☐

v) One enzyme can speed up a lot of different reactions. ☐ ☐

b) Write the correct version of each false sentence below.

....

....

....

c) Where in a **plant cell** are the enzymes found that are involved in:

i) aerobic respiration?

....

ii) photosynthesis?

....

Module B4 — The Processes of Life

DNA — Making Proteins

Q1   The following questions are about **DNA**.

a)   What name is given to the **shape** of a DNA molecule?

....

b)   How many different bases make up the DNA structure?

....

c)   Which bases pair up together?

....

Q2   Tick the boxes to show whether the following statements are **true** or **false**.   **True False**

a)   Genes are sections of DNA that code for specific proteins.   ☐ ☐

b)   Each amino acid is coded for by a set of four base pairs.   ☐ ☐

c)   DNA is found in the cytoplasm of plant and animal cells.   ☐ ☐

d)   Proteins are made in the cytoplasm of plant and animal cells.   ☐ ☐

e)   Messenger RNA carries information from the DNA into the cytoplasm.   ☐ ☐

f)   Messenger RNA molecules have two strands.   ☐ ☐

Q3   The order of bases in a gene determines the **sequence** of **amino acids** in a protein.

a)   i)   On the section of DNA shown complete the lower sequence of bases.

A G G C T A G C C A A T C G C C G A A G C T C A
| | | | | | | | | | | | | | | | | | | | | |
T C C G A T C G G T T A G C G

ii) Calculate how many **amino acids** this section of DNA codes for.

....

b)   Using the information in the table complete the amino acid sequence for the following messenger RNA sequence. The first two have been done for you.

CGAAAGGCGGAAGAAAAGGCGGCG

..2.. ..3.. ....

Triplet	Amino Acid Reference Number
GCG	1
CGA	2
AAG	3
GAA	4

Cell Division — Mitosis

Q1   Complete the following passage using some of the words below.

> genetically   four   egg   copies
> two   growth   damaged   parent

Mitosis is where a cell divides into .... cells. These new cells are

.... identical to each other and the .... cell.

Before a cell divides, it .... its DNA. Organisms use mitosis

for .... and to replace .... cells.

Q2   Tick the boxes to show whether the following statements are **true** or **false**.

                                               True   **False**

a) As a cell grows the number of organelles increases. ☐ ☐

b) Before mitosis the chromosomes are copied so that the cell has four copies of its DNA. ☐ ☐

c) When chromosomes are copied the strands of a DNA molecule separate so that new strands can form next to them. ☐ ☐

Q3   The following diagram shows the different stages of **mitosis**. Write a short description to explain each stage. The first one has been done for you.

> The cell's DNA duplicates and forms X-shaped chromosomes. Each arm of a chromosome is exactly the same as the other.

a) ....
....

b) ....
....

c) ....
....

Cell Division — Meiosis

Q1   Tick the boxes below to show which statements are true of **mitosis**, **meiosis** or **both**.

	Mitosis	Meiosis
a) Halves the number of chromosomes.	☐	☐
b) Is a type of cell division.	☐	☐
c) Forms cells that are genetically different.	☐	☐
d) In humans, it only happens in the reproductive organs.	☐	☐

Q2   The diagram shows the formation of a **zygote** from two **gametes**. Complete the table below.

Gametes

A   +   B

Sigh.

Zygote

C

	What is it?	Number of chromosomes	Formed by
A			meiosis
B		23	
C	fertilised egg cell		fertilisation

Q3   During sexual reproduction, two **gametes** combine to form a new individual.

a)   What are gametes?

....

b)   Explain why gametes have **half** the usual number of chromosomes.

....

....

Top Tips: I've tried for ages to come up with a good way of remembering which is mitosis and which is meiosis. Unfortunately I got stuck at "My toes(ies) grow(sies)...", which is rather lame if I may say so myself. I hope for your sake you come up with something better. Good luck...

Animal Development

Q1 Use the words provided to complete the passage below.

stem cells	embryo	eight
meiosis	specialised	tissues	mitosis

Once an egg is fertilised it divides by .... and forms an

...., made up of embryonic ....

These cells can divide to produce any type of .... cell.

After the .... cell stage the cells form

.... and organs.

Q2 Some **stem cells** are extracted from a **cloned** embryo. Number the stages in the correct order to show how a cloned embryo is produced. The first one has been done for you.

......1...... Take an egg cell.

.... An embryo forms.

.... Insert the nucleus from a body cell of an adult you want to clone.

.... Remove the genetic material.

.... The inactive genes in the body cell's nucleus are switched on under the right conditions.

.... Extract embryonic stem cells.

Q3 Describe how **stem cells** are currently used in **medicine**.

....

....

Q4 How are **embryonic** stem cells different from **adult** stem cells?

....

....

Plant Development

Q1 Plants can produce cells which are **unspecialised**.

a) Circle the name of the **plant tissue** that produces unspecialised cells.

auxins   mericells   cuttings   meristems

b) Tick the boxes to show whether the following statements are **true** or **false**.

	True	False

i) The plant tissue that produces unspecialised cells can be found in roots and shoots. ☐ ☐

ii) As the plant ages the unspecialised cells lose their ability to become any type of cell. ☐ ☐

iii) Any kind of plant cell can be made by the unspecialised cells. ☐ ☐

c) Give two examples of **tissue** that unspecialised plant cells can form.

1. .... 2. ....

Q2 Barry is investigating the effect of rooting powder which contains **plant hormones** on the growth of the roots in some **identical plant cuttings**. His measurements are shown in the table.

a) What are plant cuttings? ....

b) Suggest the name of the plant hormones in the rooting powder. ....

The table shows the effect of the plant hormones concentration on root growth over a week.

Concentration of plant hormones (parts per million)	0	0.001	0.01	0.1	1
Increase in root length (mm)	6	12	8	3	1

c) Plot a **bar chart** below of the increase in root length against the concentration of plant hormones.

d) What do the results suggest is the **best concentration** of plant hormones to encourage growth?

....

Top Tips: You often hear about athletes being caught by random drugs tests for using hormones to beef themselves up a bit — I've never heard of any gardeners having their prize vegetable carted off for a random plant hormone test though. Hmmmm...

Phototropism and Auxins

Q1 **Phototropism** is necessary for the survival of plants.

a) Explain what **positive** and **negative** phototropism are.

....

....

b) Explain why positive and negative phototropism is needed for a plant to **survive**.

Positive phototropism: ....

....

Negative phototropism: ....

....

Q2 Three **plant shoots** (A, B and C) were exposed to a **light stimulus**.
The diagram shows the shape of each shoot before and after the experiment.

a) Which part of the plant shoot is **most sensitive** to light?

....

b) Which plant **hormones** control growth near this part?

....

c) On **each** shoot in the diagram, shade in the region that contains the **most** of this hormone.

The black cap and sleeve keep light out.

Q3 Two shoot tips were removed from young plants. Agar blocks **soaked in auxins** were placed on the **cut ends** of the **shoots** as shown in the diagram, and they were placed in the dark. The auxins **soak** into the stem where the block touches it.

a) Describe the expected responses of shoots A and B to this treatment.

i) Shoot A ....

ii) Shoot B ....

b) Explain your answers.

i) Shoot A ....

....

....

ii) Shoot B ....

....

Module B5 — Growth and Development

Mixed Questions — Module B5

Q1   Cell division occurs by **meiosis** and **mitosis**.

Draw a line to connect the terms to their descriptions.

| Mitosis... | ...is where cell division produces two new cells that are identical to each other and the parent cell. |

| Meiosis... | ...is where cell division produces gametes. |

Q2   The **bases** in DNA always pair up in the **same** way.

Complete the diagram below to show which **bases** will form the complementary strand of DNA.

A	C	T	G	C	A	A	T	G
......	......	......	......	......	......	......	......	......

Q3   Number the statements below to show the correct order of the stages involved in making a **protein**.

☐ Amino acids are joined together to make a protein.

☐ Messenger RNA moves out of the nucleus.

☐ A molecule of messenger RNA is made using DNA as a template.

☐ The DNA strand unzips.

☐ Messenger RNA joins with an organelle that makes proteins.

Organelles are structures inside cells.

Q4   Norbert takes a **cutting** from a part of his ornamental houseplant that contains **meristems**. He's giving the cutting to his aunt so she can grow the plant for herself.

a) Explain why it's important for a cutting to contain meristems.

....

....

b) Circle the correct word to complete the sentences below.

i) Plant cuttings can grow into a **seed** / **clone** of the parent plant.

ii) Cuttings are usually taken from plants with **desirable** / **unpleasant** features.

c) Explain why cuttings are grown with **rooting powder**.

....

....

Mixed Questions — Module B5

Q5 Some parts of plants grow in response to **light**.

a) Give the name of this response.

....

b) Decide whether the following statements are **true** or **false**.

    i) Plant shoots grow away from light.

    ii) Plant roots grow towards light.

    iii) Positive phototropism ensures that roots grow deep into the soil for nutrients.

    iv) If the tip of a shoot is removed, the shoot may stop growing.

True   False

c) Write the correct version of the **false** statements.

....

....

....

....

Q6 Scientists are conducting research into using **embryonic stem cells** to produce tissues and organs.

a) **i)** What is a **tissue**?

....

    ii) What is an **organ**?

....

I've never heard anyone play the organ so badly.

Tissue?

b) Suggest a reason why some people think it's **unethical** to use embryonic stem cells for research.

....

....

c) Circle the correct word from each pair to complete the passage below.

> **Some** / **All** of the body cells in an organism contain **the same** / **different** genes and most
>
> of the genes are switched **off** / **on**. This is because body cells only need to produce the
>
> specific **proteins** / **DNA** they need to function. But in **stem** / **liver** cells any gene can be
>
> switched **off** / **on** during their development. The genes that are active determine
>
> the **number** / **type** of cells they specialise into.

Module B5 — Growth and Development

The Nervous System

Q1 Complete the following passage using the words from the box.

environment	hormonal	change
receptors	multicellular	nervous

A stimulus is any .... in the .... of
an organism, for example a drop in air temperature. Stimuli are detected by
.... in the .... system. This system,
along with the .... system, developed as
.... organisms evolved.

Q2 The **CNS** makes up part of the **nervous system**.

a) What do the letters **CNS** stand for?

....

b) What is the **function** of the CNS?

....

c) On the diagram label the parts that make up the CNS.

d) What is the role of the **peripheral** nervous system (PNS)?

....

....

e) What type of neurones:

i) carry information **to** the CNS? ....

ii) carry instructions **from** the CNS? ....

Q3 Complete the diagram below to show the pathway of information through the nervous system.

Stimulus						Response

The Nervous System

Q4 **Receptors** and **effectors** are important cells in the nervous system.

a) What is the role of effectors?

....

b) What are receptors?

....

c) Put the words below into the correct columns in the table to show the different types of effectors
and receptors, and the different **organs** they form part of.

~~taste buds~~   glands   the eye   muscle cells

hormone secreting cells   ~~the tongue~~   muscles   light receptor cells

	Example	Make up part of...
Receptor	taste buds	the tongue
Effector		

Q5 Jamie was cooking his mum some tea when he accidentally picked up
a **hot** saucepan. Jamie **instantly** dropped the pan back onto the hob.

Put numbers in the boxes so that the following statements are in the
correct order to describe how Jamie's nervous system responded to
him picking up the hot pan. The first one has been done for you.

☐ Some of the muscles in Jamie's hand contract, causing him
to drop the pan.

1 Temperature receptors in Jamie's hand detect the increase in
temperature.

☐ Impulses travel along a motor neurone.

☐ Impulses travel along a sensory neurone.

☐ The information is processed by the spinal cord.

Neurones and Synapses

Q1 The diagram below shows a typical **neurone**.

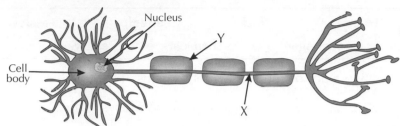

a) How does information travel along the neurone?

   ....

b) Complete the following sentences by circling the correct word in each pair.

   > Structure X is the **synapse** / **axon** of the neurone. It's made from the neurone's
   >
   > **cytoplasm** / **nucleus** stretched into a long fibre and surrounded by a cell **membrane** / **wall**.

c) Name the part labelled **Y** and describe its function.

   ....

   ....

Q2 The neurones in the body **aren't directly connected** together — there are small **gaps** between them.

a) What **name** is given to the small gap between two neurones?

   ....

b) Information is transmitted across the gap using **transmitter chemicals**. Explain how this works.

   ....

   ....

   ....

Q3 Some **drugs** affect **transmission** of impulses around the nervous system.

   Describe an effect **ecstasy** (MDMA) has on the synapses in the brain and say why the drug is often described as having 'mood-enhancing effects'.

   ....

   ....

   ....

<u>*Neurones and Synapses*</u>

Q4   Complete the passage below using the words provided.

blood	fast	effector	slow
oestrogen	chemical	electrical	neurones

Animals have two types of communication systems. Hormonal communication systems

transmit .... signals called hormones (e.g ....).

Hormones are carried in the .... and tend to cause .... ,

long-lasting effects in the body. Nervous communication systems are made up of cells

called .... These cells link receptor cells (e.g. in the eyes) with

.... cells (e.g. in muscles). Nerve cells carry ....

impulses for .... , short-lived responses.

Q5   Brian is depressed. His doctor is considering prescribing Brian **PROZAC®**, so he gives him a leaflet about the drug. Read the passage below and answer the questions that follow.

- PROZAC® is a drug that is sometimes prescribed to people who are suffering from depression.
- PROZAC® works by blocking the sites where the neurotransmitter serotonin is removed.
- This means that the serotonin concentration increases in a person's synapses, which has a mood-enhancing effect.

a)   PROZAC® and serotonin are both present in the synapses of patients who have taken the drug. Explain why serotonin triggers a **nerve impulse** in neurones, but PROZAC® doesn't.

....

....

b)   Name **one** other drug that has the same effect on **serotonin concentration** as PROZAC®.

....

c)   Name **one** other drug that affects the transmission of impulses across synapses.

....

> **<u>*Top Tips:*</u>**   Hopefully you've got your head around what the nervous system is and how it works.   It's really worthwhile making sure you're happy with answering questions on the basics — otherwise you might struggle with some of the topics that pop up later on in the section.

Reflexes

Q1   Circle the correct word(s) in each pair to complete the following sentences.

a)   Reflexes happen more **quickly** / **slowly** than other responses.

b)   The neurones involved in reflexes go through the **back bone** / **spinal cord** or **an unconscious** / **a conscious** part of the brain.

c)   Reflexes are **voluntary** / **involuntary**.

d)   The nervous pathway of a reflex is called a reflex **arc** / **ellipse**.

e)   An impulse always travels along **the same** / **a different** route through a reflex pathway.

Q2   List three reflexes that **newborn babies** have.

1. ....

2. ....

3. ....

Q3   **Reflexes** produce many important responses. Tick the boxes below to show whether the following statements are **true** or **false**.

	True	False
a) The pupil reflex focuses light onto the retina to help with vision.	☐	☐
b) Reflex actions help simple animals to respond to some changes in their environment in a way that helps them survive.	☐	☐
c) Reflex actions can help simple animals to find food and hide from predators.	☐	☐
d) Simple animals don't rely entirely on reflexes.	☐	☐

Q4   When you touch something **hot** with a finger you **automatically** pull the finger away. This is an example of a **reflex action**.

Complete the passage using words from the box below.

motor	sensory	receptors	effector	relay	stimulus	CNS

When the .... is detected by .... in the finger an

impulse is sent along a .... neurone to a .... neurone

in the .... The impulse is passed to a .... neurone,

which carries the impulse to the ....

Modifying and Learning Reflexes

Q1   Read the passage about **Pavlov** and answer the questions that follow.

> Pavlov's most famous experiment looked at conditioning in dogs. The experiment was based on the observation that dogs salivated every time they smelt food. In his experiment a bell was rung just before the dogs were fed. Eventually he noticed that the dogs would salivate when the bell was rung even if they couldn't smell food.

a)   From the passage, identify the:

   i) primary stimulus   ....

   ii) secondary stimulus   ....

   iii) unconditioned reflex   ....

   iv) conditioned reflex   ....

b)   Which reflex, conditioned or unconditioned, has been learnt?

   ....

c)   Complete the following sentence by circling the correct words.

> In a conditioned reflex the final response has
>
> **a direct connection** / **no direct connection** to the secondary stimulus.

Q2   Birds can **learn** to reject insects with certain colourings — this is a **conditioned reflex**.

a)   Put the following statements in order to show how a conditioned reflex can increase a bird's chances of survival. The first one has been done for you.

   ☐   The bird spots a red coloured caterpillar and avoids it.

   ☐   The bird increases its chances of survival by avoiding the caterpillar and being poisoned.

   ☐ `1`   A bird spots a red coloured caterpillar. It swoops down, catches and eats the caterpillar.

   ☐   The bird learns to associate feeling unwell with the red colour.

   ☐   The bird feels unwell because of poisons in the insect.

b)   In this example, what is the **primary** stimulus?

   ....

Q3   Give one example of when it would be useful to **modify** a reflex response and describe in terms of neurones how the reflex arc is modified.

   ....

   ....

Brain Development and Learning

Q1 Tick the boxes to show whether each statement is **true** or **false**.

	True	False
	☐	☐

a) The brain contains around one million neurones. ☐ ☐

b) Complex animals with a brain are able to learn by experience. ☐ ☐

c) The brain coordinates complex behaviour such as social behaviour. ☐ ☐

d) Humans have evolved a smaller brain than other animals, which gives us a survival advantage. ☐ ☐

Q2 Complete the passage using words from the box below.

more	experience	unconnected	network
stimulated	developed	trillions	formed

Most of the neurone connections in a newborn baby's brain are not yet

...., so the brain is only partly ....

Every new .... causes the brain to become ....

developed. When neurones in the brain are .... they branch out,

forming connections between cells that were previously ....

This forms a massive .... of neurones with ....

of different routes for impulses to travel down.

Q3 Sarah and Sophie both play the **piano**. Sarah has been **practising** all week but Sophie **hasn't practised at all**. The girls' piano teacher, Mr Fudge, compliments Sarah on her performance but tells Sophie that he thinks she needs to practise more next week.

Explain why some skills can be **learnt** through **repetition**.

....

....

....

....

Top Tips: Hopefully now you'll understand the science behind the phrase 'practice makes perfect'. If that's the case, you should also understand why it's really important to keep going over stuff when you're revising — it's one of the best ways to get stuff stored away in your brain.

Learning Skills and Behaviour

Q1 Explain why **complex animals**, such as humans, are able to **adapt** to new situations better than **simple animals**, such as insects.

....

....

Q2 Read the two case studies about **feral children** below and answer the questions that follow.

Isabelle was discovered in 1938 at the age of about six. She'd spent most of her life locked in a darkened room with her mother who was deaf and unable to speak. Isabelle was unable to walk and she had the mental age of a nineteen-month old child. She rapidly learnt to speak and write. By the age of eight Isabelle had reached a 'normal' level and was eventually able to go to school, participating in all activities with other children.

Eleven-year old Tissa was discovered in 1973 in Sri Lanka. When he was caught he showed many animal characteristics, such as walking on all fours, snarling at humans and yelping. Tissa was taken into care, and although he learned to smile and to eat with his hands, he never learned how to speak.

a) Explain why Isabelle couldn't speak when she was discovered.

....

b) What do the case studies above suggest about language development in children? Use evidence to justify your answer.

....

....

....

Q3 Hew has been in a **car accident**. Bruising on his **head** suggests that he took a nasty blow during the crash. The doctors are also concerned because he's having difficulty speaking and is unable to remember simple facts.

a) What part of Hew's **brain** might have been **damaged**?

....

b) Name two other things that this part of the brain is important for.

1. ....

2. ....

Top Tips: Language development isn't the only thing that has to happen before a certain age — balance and hearing also rely on early experiences. It's the same for other animals too — some birds never learn the proper bird song for their species if they're kept in isolation when they're young.

Module B6 — Brain and Mind

Studying the Brain

Q1   Studying the brain can be useful for a number of reasons, for example in the **diagnosis** of people with brain disorders such as Parkinson's disease. Give **three methods** used by scientists to **map** the regions of the **brain**.

1. ....

2. ....

3. ....

Q2   What is **memory**?

....

Q3   There are a number of things that can influence how humans remember information.

a) Jerry is trying to remember two phone numbers:

A. 01951 845217 and B. 01234 543210

Which number, A or B, is Jerry most likely to remember? Give a reason for your answer.

....

....

b) If **strong stimuli** are associated with information it can help people to remember it. Give **three** of these stimuli.

1. ....   2. ....   3. ....

c) Give **one** other method used by humans to make them **more likely** to remember information.

....

Q4 a) Complete the diagram using the words below to illustrate the **multi-store model** of memory.

short-term memory   long-term memory   repetition   retrieval   forgotten

b) 'The multi-store model offers a complete explanation of how human memory works.'

Is this statement **true** or **false**? ....

Mixed Questions — Module B6

Q1 a) What is a **stimulus**?

....

b) Which of the following types of cell can **detect stimuli**? Circle the correct answer.

effectors	receptors

neurones

c) What type of cells **receive** impulses from **motor neurones**?

....

d) Briefly describe the structure and function of the **peripheral nervous system** (PNS).

....

....

Q2 Gavin accidentally inhaled some pepper and **sneezed**.
A sneeze is an example of a **reflex**.

a) Give two other examples of **adult** human reflexes.

1. ....

2. ....

b) Put the following statements in order to describe the path of a reflex arc.
The first one has been done for you.

☐ The impulse is passed along a relay neurone.

☐ An impulse is sent along a sensory neurone to the CNS.

☐ The impulse is sent along a motor neurone.

☐ The impulse reaches an effector, which reacts to the stimulus.

[1] A stimulus is detected by receptor cells.

c) Explain why **electrical nerve impulses**, and not **hormones**, are used for reflexes.

....

....

Module B6 — Brain and Mind

Mixed Questions — Module B6

Q3 The diagram below shows two **nerve cells**.

a) Complete the diagram by adding **labels** in the spaces provided.

i) ....

ii) ....

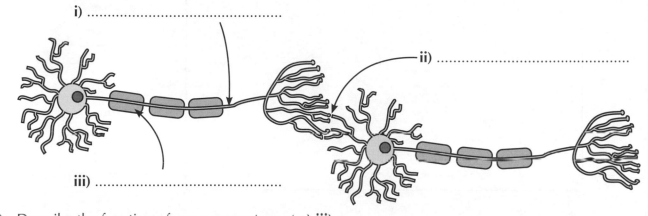

iii) ....

b) Describe the function of your answer to part **a) iii)**.

....

....

Q4 Complete the passage using the words below.

repeated	harder	practised	strengthened	more

When experiences are .... the pathways that the nerve impulses travel

down become .... These pathways are ....

likely to transmit impulses than others — this makes some activities much easier if you've

.... them a lot. After the age of ten, the pathways that aren't used as

often die off. This is why it's .... for older people to learn new things.

Q5 Stephen picks up his **hot** cup of tea.

a) Describe how the reflex that would normally make Stephen drop the cup can be **modified**.

....

....

b) Explain why it's **useful** for Stephen to modify his reflex response in this situation.

....

Atoms

Q1 Draw a diagram of a **helium atom** in the space provided and label each type of **particle** on your diagram.

Helium has 2 of each type of particle.

Q2 **Complete** this table.

Particle	Mass	Charge
Proton	1	
		0
Electron	0.0005	

Q3 **Complete** the following sentences.

a) Neutral atoms have a charge of ....

b) In atoms the electrons are arranged in .... around the nucleus.

c) A neutral atom has the same number of .... and ....

d) The number of .... in an atom tells you what element it is.

e) Protons and neutrons are both found in the ....

Q4 Complete the table below to show the number of **protons** and **electrons** in these atoms.

element	electrons	protons
magnesium	12	
carbon		6
oxygen		

Use a periodic table to help you with this question.

Chemical Equations

Q1   Which of the following equations are **balanced** correctly? Tick the correct boxes.

	Correctly balanced	Incorrectly balanced
a) $H_2 + Cl_2 \rightarrow 2HCl$	☐	☐
b) $CuO + HCl \rightarrow CuCl_2 + H_2O$	☐	☐
c) $N_2 + H_2 \rightarrow NH_3$	☐	☐
d) $CuO + H_2 \rightarrow Cu + H_2O$	☐	☐
e) $CaCO_3 \rightarrow CaO + CO_2$	☐	☐

Alice and Bob were incorrectly balanced.

Q2   Here is the equation for the formation of **carbon monoxide** in a poorly ventilated gas fire. It is **not** balanced correctly.

$$C + O_2 \rightarrow CO$$

Circle the **correctly balanced** version of this equation.

$$C + O_2 \rightarrow CO_2$$

$$C + O_2 \rightarrow 2CO$$

$$2C + O_2 \rightarrow 2CO$$

Q3   **Sodium** (Na) reacts with **water** (H_2O) to produce **sodium hydroxide** (NaOH) and **hydrogen** (H_2).

a) What are the **reactants** and the **products** in this reaction?

Reactants: ....   Products: ....

b) Write the **word equation** for this reaction.

....

c) Write the **balanced symbol equation** for the reaction.

....

d) What state symbol would be used in the equations above for:

i)   water? ....   ii) hydrogen gas? ....

Top Tips: The most important thing to remember with balancing equations is that you **can't** change the **little numbers** — if you do that then you'll change the substance into something completely different. Right, now that I've given you that little gem of knowledge, you can carry on with the rest. Just take your time and work through everything logically.

Chemical Equations

Q4 Write out the balanced **symbol** equations for the picture equations below (some of which are unbalanced).

a) + →

You can draw more pictures to help you balance the unbalanced ones.

b) + → Li O Li

c) Mg O C O + H Cl → Cl Mg Cl + H O H + O C O

d) Li + H O H / H O H → Li O H + H H

Q5 Add **one** number to each of these equations so that they are **correctly balanced**.

a) .... CuO + ... HBr → .... $CuBr_2$ + ... H_2O

b) .... H_2 + ... Br_2 → .... HBr

You need to have 2 bromines and 2 hydrogens on the left-hand side.

c) .... Mg + ... O_2 → $2MgO$

d) $2NaOH$ + ... H_2SO_4 → .... Na_2SO_4 + ... H_2O

Q6 **Balance** these equations by adding in numbers.

If a line doesn't need a number, just leave it blank.

a) .... $NaOH$ + ... $AlBr_3$ → .... $NaBr$ + ... $Al(OH)_3$

b) .... $FeCl_2$ + ... Cl_2 → .... $FeCl_3$

c) .... N_2 + ... H_2 → .... NH_3

d) .... Fe + ... O_2 → .... Fe_2O_3

e) .... NH_3 + ... O_2 → .... NO + ... H_2O

$Fe_2O_3 + 3CO → 2Fe + 3CO_2$

Line Spectrums

Q1 A scientist is carrying out a **flame test** to identify the **metals** in three different compounds.

Choose the correct word from each pair to complete the following sentences.

a) Some elements emit distinctive .... when ....

cooled   heated   colours   smells

b) Three elements which can be identified in a flame test

are lithium, sodium and ....

bromine   gold   argon   potassium

You have one hour to complete the test starting now.

FLAME TEST 1 HOUR

Q2 a) Use the words in the box to complete the passage about **line spectrums**. Some words may be used more than once.

light   element   electrons   elements   excited   electron   line

When an atom is heated its .... become ....

and release energy as ....

The wavelengths of .... emitted can be recorded as a

.... spectrum. Different .... emit different

wavelengths of .... due to their different ....

arrangements. This means that each .... will produce a different

.... spectrum, allowing them to be identified.

b) As well as to help identify elements, what else have line spectrums been used for?

....

Q3 Name the practical technique used to obtain line spectrums. Circle the correct answer.

chromatography   calorimetry   spectroscopy

Top Tips: I don't know why atoms get so excited at the prospect of being stuck in a hot flame — it certainly doesn't appeal to me. There's no accounting for some tastes... Anyway, line spectrums aren't as tricky as they might seem at first. Stick at it — they could easily come up in the exam — and you'll be passing with, errr... flying colours...

History of the Periodic Table

Q1 Which of the following statements about **Mendeleev's** Table of Elements are **true** and which are **false**? Tick the correct boxes.

		True	False
a)	Early attempts to link chemical properties to relative atomic mass were dismissed by the scientific community.	☐	☐
b)	Mendeleev arranged the elements in order of increasing atomic number.	☐	☐
c)	Mendeleev was able to predict the properties of undiscovered elements.	☐	☐
d)	Elements with similar properties appeared in the same rows.	☐	☐

Q2 Describe how **Döbereiner** chose elements for his **triads**.

....

Q3 When **Newlands** arranged the known elements in order of **atomic mass** in 1864, the first three rows were as shown.

	1					**2**
H	Li	Be	B	C	N	O
F	Na	Mg	Al	Si	P	S
Cl	K	Ca	Cr	Ti	Mn	Fe

a) In which of the two highlighted groups do the elements have similar properties? ....

b) This arrangement of elements was known as 'Newlands' Octaves'. Why did Newlands arrange the elements in rows of seven?

....

c) Why didn't helium and neon appear in Newlands' table?

....

Q4 Mendeleev left **gaps** in his Table of Elements to keep elements with similar properties in the same groups. He predicted that elements would eventually be discovered to fill the gaps. For example, he predicted the discovery of an element that would fill a gap in his Group 4 and called it '**ekasilicon**'.

Element	Density g/cm³
carbon	2.27
silicon	2.33
'ekasilicon'	
tin	7.29
lead	11.34

The table shows the **densities** of known elements in this group.

a) 'Ekasilicon' was eventually discovered and given another name. Use the information in the table to decide which of the elements below is 'ekasilicon'. Circle your choice.

palladium, 12.02 g/cm³   **germanium, 5.32 g/cm³**   **beryllium, 1.85 g/cm³**   **copper, 8.93 g/cm³**

b) i) What did Mendeleev's arrangement have **in common** with Newlands' earlier attempt?

....

....

....

ii) What was the main **difference** between their approaches?

....

Module C4 — Chemical Patterns

The Modern Periodic Table

Q1   Use a **periodic table** to help you answer the following questions.

a)   Name one element in the same period as silicon.   ....

b)   Name one element in the same group as potassium.   ....

c)   Name one element that is in group 7.   ....

d)   Name an element with one electron in its outer shell.   ....

Q2   **Complete** this table.

Name	Symbol	Relative atomic mass	Proton number
Iron	Fe	56	
	Pb	207	
Xenon			54
Copper			

Q3   Select from these **elements** to answer the following questions.

iodine   nickel   silicon   sodium   radon   krypton   calcium

a)   Which two elements are in the same group?   .... and ....

b)   Name two elements which are in Period 3.   .... and ....

c)   Name a transition metal.   ....

d)   Name a non-metal that is not in Group 0.   ....

You can use a periodic table to help with all the questions on pages 37-38.

Q4   Choose from the words below to fill in the blanks in each sentence.

left-hand	right-hand	horizontal	similar	different
vertical	group	period	increasing	decreasing

a)   A group in the periodic table is a .... line of elements.

b)   Elements in the same .... have the same number of electrons in their outer shells.

c)   Elements in the periodic table are arranged in order of .... proton number.

d)   Non-metals are on the .... side of the periodic table.

e)   Elements in the same group have .... properties.

The Modern Periodic Table

Q5 Tick the correct boxes to show whether these statements are **true** or **false**. **True False**

a) The rows in the periodic table are also known as periods.

b) Each column in the periodic table contains elements with similar properties.

c) The periodic table is made up of all the known compounds.

d) An element's group number tells you how many electrons it has in its outer shell.

e) Each new period in the periodic table represents another full shell of electrons.

Q6 Argon is an extremely **unreactive** gas. Use the periodic table to give the names of two more gases that you would expect to have similar properties to argon.

My property in the country.

Ar

1. ....

2. ....

Q7 Fill in the **missing information** in the table below using a periodic table.

Element	Relative atomic mass	Number of protons	Number of electrons	Number of neutrons
Potassium	39		19	
Phosphorous	31	15		
Neon		10		10

Q8 Elements in the same group undergo **similar reactions**.

a) Tick the pairs of elements that would undergo similar reactions.

A potassium and rubidium ☐ C calcium and oxygen ☐

B helium and fluorine ☐ D nitrogen and arsenic ☐

b) Boron and aluminium are in the same group. State whether each is a **metal** or a **non-metal**.

Boron: ....

Aluminium: ....

Top Tips: The periodic table does more than just tell you the names and symbols of all the elements. You can get some other pretty important information from it too. For starters, it's all arranged in a useful pattern which means that elements with similar properties form columns.

Electron Shells

Q1 a) Tick the boxes to show whether each statement is **true** or **false**.

True **False**

i) Electrons occupy shells (energy levels) in atoms. ☐ ☐

ii) The highest energy levels are always filled first. ☐ ☐

iii) Elements in Group 0 have a full outer shell of electrons. ☐ ☐

iv) Reactive elements have full outer shells. ☐ ☐

v) Each shell fills with electrons as you go across a period. ☐ ☐

vi) An element's electron arrangement determines its chemical properties. ☐ ☐

b) Write out corrected versions of the **false** statements.

....

....

Q2 Describe **two** things that are wrong with this diagram.

1. ....

....

2. ....

....

Q3 Write out the **electron configurations** of the following elements.

Use a periodic table to help you with this question.

a) Beryllium ....

d) Calcium ....

b) Oxygen ....

e) Aluminium ....

c) Silicon ....

f) Argon ....

Q4 **Chlorine** has an atomic number of 17.

a) What is its electron configuration? ....

b) Draw the electrons on the shells in the diagram.

Cl

Ionic Bonding

Q1   Fill in the gaps in the sentences below by choosing the correct words from the box.

protons	charged particles	repelled by
electrons	ions	attracted to	neutral particles

a)   In ionic bonding atoms lose or gain .... to form ....

b)   Ions are ....

c)   Ions with opposite charges are strongly .... each other.

Q2   Use this **diagram** to help you answer the following questions.

a)   How many electrons does **chlorine** need to gain to get a full outer shell of electrons? ....

b)   What is the charge on a **sodium ion**? ....

c)   What is the chemical formula of **sodium chloride**? ....

Q3   Tick the correct boxes to show whether the following statements are **true** or **false**.

True False

a)   The ions in an ionic compound are arranged in a lattice formation.

b)   When an ionic compound dissolves the ions become more closely packed together.

c)   When ionic compounds are molten or dissolved they can conduct electricity, because the ions are free to move around.

d)   A compound made up of a metal and a non-metal will conduct electricity when it's molten — this is evidence that it's made up of ions.

e)   Compounds formed between group 1 and group 7 elements are covalent compounds.

f)   A crystal of a solid ionic compound is made up of a single giant lattice of ions.

Q4   Chlorine (Cl) is a **group 7** element. It forms a **-1** ion when it reacts with potassium (K).

Explain how chlorine becomes a -1 ion. The electronic structure of chlorine is shown below.

....

....

....

Ions and Formulas

Q1 Here are some **elements** and the **ions** they form:

beryllium, Be^{2+}　　　potassium, K^+　　　iodine, I^-　　　sulfur, S^{2-}

Write down the formulas of four compounds that can be made using just these ions.

1. ....

2. ....

3. ....

4. ....

Make sure the charges on the ions balance.

Q2 Find the charge on the **chloride ion** in calcium chloride.

The formula is $CaCl_2$ and the charge on the calcium ion is 2^+.

....

....

Q3 Use the table to find the **formulas** of the following compounds.

Positive Ions		Negative Ions	
Potassium	K^+	Fluoride	F^-
Calcium	Ca^{2+}	Bromide	Br^-
Iron(II)	Fe^{2+}	Carbonate	CO_3^{2-}
Iron(III)	Fe^{3+}	Sulfate	SO_4^{2-}

a) potassium bromide　　...

b) iron(II) sulfate　　...

c) calcium fluoride　　...

Q4 **Aluminium** forms ions with a 3^+ charge. **Oxygen** forms ions with a 2^- charge

a) Find the formula of **aluminium oxide**.

....

b) The formula of **magnesium oxide** is MgO. What is the charge on a **magnesium ion**?

....

c) The formula of **aluminium hydroxide** is $Al(OH)_3$. What is the charge on a **hydroxide ion**?

....

Module C4 — Chemical Patterns

Group 1 — The Alkali Metals

Q1 **Sodium**, **potassium** and **lithium** are all alkali metals.

a) Highlight the location of the alkali metals on this periodic table.

b) Put sodium, potassium and lithium in order of increasing reactivity and state their symbols.

least reactive ....

....

most reactive ....

Q2 Complete the following sentence with one of the phrases below.

Alkali metal atoms all have .... in their outer shell.

1 electron   **4 electrons**   **7 electrons**   **8 electrons**

Q3 Giles has a small lump of **sodium**. He cuts it in half with a sharp knife.

a) Describe the sodium's appearance after it was first cut.

....

b) Describe the appearance of the sodium when it has been left to stand in the air for a short time.

....

c) Explain your answer to part **b)**.

....

Q4 The table shows the **melting points** of some Group 1 metals.

a) Would you expect the melting point of **caesium** to be higher or lower than **rubidium**? Explain your answer.

....

....

Element	Melting point (°C)
Li	181
Na	98
K	63
Rb	39
Cs	?

b) Complete the following sentences:

i) **As you move down Group 1, the reactivity of the atoms** ....

ii) **As you move up Group 1, the density of the atoms** ....

Group 1 — The Alkali Metals

Q5   Potassium is an **alkali metal**.

a)   Complete the symbol equation for the reaction of potassium with chlorine.

$$2\,K_{(s)}\ +\ Cl_{2\,(g)}\ \rightarrow\ \dots\dots\dots\dots\dots\dots\dots$$

b)   Describe the appearance of the product(s).

....

c)   Potassium and sodium both belong to Group 1. Why do they have similar properties?

....

Q6   Circle the correct words to complete the passage below.

> Sodium is a soft metal with **one** / **two** electron(s) in its outer shell. It reacts vigorously
> with water, producing **sodium dioxide** / **sodium hydroxide** and **hydrogen** / **oxygen** gas.

Q7   Archibald put a piece of **lithium** into a beaker of water.

a)   Describe the reaction that occurred.

....

b)   After the reaction had finished, Archibald tested the water with universal indicator. **"squeaky pop!"**
What colour change would he see, and why?

....

....

> In acidic solutions, universal
> indicator turns red. In alkaline
> solutions, it turns purple.

c)   Write a **balanced symbol equation** for the reaction, including state symbols.

....

d)   **i)** Write a **word equation** for the reaction between sodium and water.

....

ii) Would you expect the reaction between sodium and water to be **more** or **less** vigorous
than the reaction between lithium and water? Explain your answer.

....

....

Top Tips: The most important thing to remember about the alkali metals is that their reactivity
increases as you move down the group. The atoms get bigger, so the outer electrons get further and
further from the nucleus. This means that they're easier to lose — so the elements are more reactive.

Group 7 — The Halogens

Q1 Draw lines to match each halogen to its correct **symbol**, **description** (at room temperature) and **reactivity**.

HALOGEN	SYMBOL	DESCRIPTION	REACTIVITY
bromine	Cl	green gas	most reactive
chlorine	I	grey solid	least reactive
fluorine	Br	orange liquid	quite reactive
iodine	F	yellow gas	very reactive

Q2 Decide whether the statements about the halogens below are **true** or **false**.

True False

a) Chlorine gas is made up of molecules which each contain three chlorine atoms. ☐ ☐

b) Iodine is less reactive than bromine because its outer electrons are further away from its nucleus. ☐ ☐

c) The halogens become darker in colour as you move down the group. ☐ ☐

d) All the halogens have one outer electron. ☐ ☐

e) All the halogens are diatomic molecules. ☐ ☐

Q3 **Iron** can be reacted with **bromine** in a fume cupboard. An **orange solid** forms on the sides of the test tube.

bromine — iron wool
HEAT

a) Name the compound formed. ....

b) Write the balanced symbol equation for the reaction between iron and bromine to form **FeBr$_3$**. Include state symbols in your answer.

....

Q4 Add the phrases to the table to show how the properties of the halogens change as you go **down** the group.

the melting points of the halogens   the reactivity of the halogens
the boiling points of the halogens

Increase(s) down the group	Decrease(s) down the group

Group 7 — The Halogens

Q5 Sodium was reacted with **bromine vapour** using the equipment shown. White crystals of a new solid were formed during the reaction.

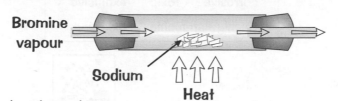

Bromine vapour

Sodium

Heat

a) Name the solid product formed.

....

b) Write a **balanced** symbol equation for the reaction.

....

c) Would you expect the above reaction to be **faster** or **slower** than a similar reaction between:

i) sodium and **iodine** vapour? Explain your answer.

....

ii) sodium and **chlorine** vapour? Explain your answer.

....

Q6 Equal volumes of **bromine water** were added to two test tubes, each containing a different **potassium halide solution**. The results are shown in the table.

SOLUTION	RESULT
potassium chloride	no colour change
potassium iodide	colour change

a) Explain these results.

....

....

....

b) Write a **balanced symbol equation** for the reaction in the potassium iodide solution.

....

c) Would you expect a reaction between:

i) bromine water and potassium astatide? ....

ii) bromine water and potassium fluoride? ....

Astatine is at the bottom of group 7.

Module C4 — Chemical Patterns

Laboratory Safety

Q1   Fill in the meaning of each hazard symbol by choosing the correct label from the box.

| corrosive | toxic | explosive |
| highly flammable | | oxidising |

a) ....

b) ....

c) ....

d) ....

e) ....

Q2   The **alkali metals** are very reactive and so must be used with great care.

a)   Explain why the alkali metals are stored under **oil**.

....

....

b)   Suggest what should be done to any apparatus that is going to come into contact with an alkali metal.

....

c)   Why must the solutions that the alkali metals form not touch the eyes or the skin?

....

Q3   The **halogens** must also be dealt with very carefully.

a)   Why must the halogens only be used inside a fume cupboard?

....

b)   Liquid bromine is **corrosive**. Explain what this means.

....

Broom
Cupboard

You're supposed
to use the
fume cupboard

Top Tips: Laboratory safety isn't something that you can afford to skim over. It's important both for your exam and for when you're working in the lab. Unfortunately it's not enough to know that a symbol means that a chemical is dangerous — you need to know how it's dangerous.

Mixed Questions — Module C4

Q1   **Sodium** is a Group 1 element with proton number 11.

a)   Use the periodic table to fill in the table below with the number of protons, neutrons and electrons in a **sodium atom**.

Number of protons	
Number of neutrons	
Number of electrons	

b)   Sodium reacts with chlorine gas (Cl_2) to form **sodium chloride**.

   i)   Describe the appearance of the sodium chloride formed.

   ....

   ii) Write a **balanced symbol equation** for this reaction, including state symbols.

   ....

c)   Sodium chloride is an **ionic compound**.

   i)   Describe the **structure** of a solid ionic compound.

   ....

   ii) Chlorine is a **Group 7** element. Describe how an **ionic bond** is formed between
   a sodium atom and an chlorine atom in sodium chloride.

   ....

   ....

   ....

Q2   **Chlorine** is a **halogen**.

a)   Write out the **electron configuration** of a chlorine atom. Use the periodic table to help you.

   ....

b)   Using your answer to part **a)**, explain why chlorine is very **reactive**.

   ....

c)   James has been given a mystery halogen known as **Halogen X**. He has to work out which element
   Halogen X is before the timer runs out and Dr. Yes blows up the Earth. Use the information below
   to work out the **identity** of Halogen X and help James save the world from the evil Dr. Yes.

   | Halogen X is toxic. |

   | Halogen X reacts with potassium bromide at
   room temperature to form an orange liquid. |

   Identity of halogen X:

   ....

   | Halogen X does not react
   with potassium fluoride. |

Chemicals in the Atmosphere

Q1 The table shows some of the **elements** and **compounds** that are found in **dry air**. Complete the table to show whether the substances are elements or compounds, give the **formula** for each substance and state their **percentage** in the atmosphere.

substance	element or compound?	formula	percentage in atmosphere
oxygen			
carbon dioxide			
argon			
nitrogen			

Q2 Choose words from the box to complete the passage below.

molecular	compounds	weak	metallic	atoms	non-metallic	strong

Most .... elements and most compounds formed from them

are .... substances. The .... within

the molecules are held together by very .... covalent bonds.

The forces of attraction between the molecules are very ....

Q3 Complete the following sentences by circling the correct option, and explain your answers.

a) The melting and boiling points of simple molecular substances are **low** / **high**.

   ....

b) Simple molecular substances **conduct** / **don't conduct** electricity.

   ....

c) Simple molecular substances are usually **gases and liquids** / **solids** at room temperature.

   ....

Q4 The table gives the **melting** and **boiling points** of some **molecular elements**. State whether each will be a **solid**, **liquid** or **gas** at **room temperature** (25 °C).

element	melting point	boiling point
fluorine	–220 °C	–188 °C
bromine	–7 °C	59 °C
iodine	114 °C	185 °C

a) fluorine ....

b) bromine ....

c) iodine ....

Covalent Bonding

Q1   Tick the boxes to say whether each statement is **true** or **false**.

True False

a)   Covalent bonding involves sharing electrons.   ☐ ☐

b)   Each covalent bond provides two extra shared electrons for each atom.   ☐ ☐

c)   Atoms form covalent bonds to gain a full outer shell of electrons.   ☐ ☐

Q2   Complete the following diagrams by adding **electrons**.
Only the **outer shells** are shown.

a)   Hydrogen (H_2)

Use • and x to show the electrons from the different atoms.

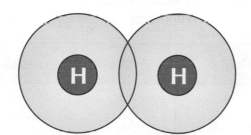

"Oi, give me that electron, big nose!"

b)   Carbon dioxide (CO_2)

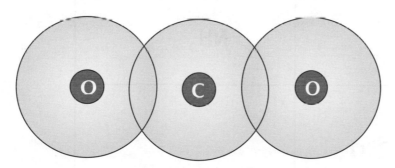

Hint — look at the groups on the periodic table that oxygen and carbon are in to work out how many electrons they have in their outer shell.

c)   Water (H_2O)

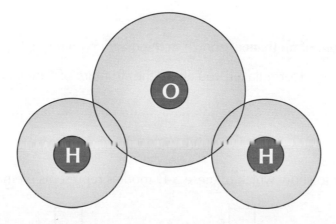

Top Tips: Atoms can bond ionically, as you'll know from page 40, or they can bond covalently. Make sure you know what covalent bonds are, and how they arise. It's really important for understanding all about the chemicals that are floating about up there in the atmosphere.

Covalent Bonding

Q3 Choose from the words in the box to complete the passage below.

electronic	positive	electrostatic	neutral	negative

In a covalent bond, the .... nuclei and the

shared .... electrons are held together by

.... attraction.

Q4 Complete the table showing the **displayed formulas** and **molecular formulas** of three compounds.

DISPLAYED FORMULA	MOLECULAR FORMULA
H | H—C—H | H	a)
b)	NH$_3$
O=S=O	c)

Q5 The **displayed formula** of **methane** is shown in the diagram on the right.

a) What **can't** the displayed formula tell you about the structure of a molecule?

....

....

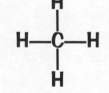

b) Tick the correct box to show which of these 3-D models represents methane.

☐ 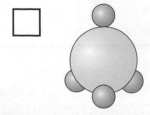   ☐ 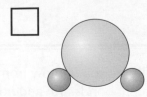   ☐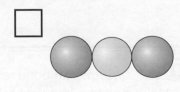

Chemicals in the Hydrosphere

Q1 Choose from the words in the box to complete the passage below.

covalent	salty	dissolved	water	ionic	salts	gases

The Earth's hydrosphere consists of all the .... on the Earth's

surface and the compounds .... in it. Many of these compounds

are ...., and are called .... It is these that

make seawater ....

Q2 Potassium chloride is an example of a **salt** found in the **sea**. Mike carries out an experiment to find out if **potassium chloride** conducts electricity. He tests the compound when it's **solid** and when it's **dissolved** in water.

a) Complete the following table of results.

	When solid	When dissolved in water
Conducts electricity?		

b) Explain your answers to part a).

....

....

....

c) State the molecular formulas for the following salts found in the sea. Use the table of positive and negative ions provided to help you.

i) Sodium sulfate ....

ii) Magnesium chloride ....

iii) Potassium bromide ....

Positive ions	Negative ions
sodium Na^+	chlorine Cl^-
potassium K^+	bromine Br^-
magnesium Mg^{2+}	sulfate SO_4^{2-}

Q3 Sodium chloride has an **ionic structure**.

a) Circle the correct words to explain why sodium chloride has a high melting point.

Sodium and chloride ions form **an irregular / a regular** lattice, which has very **strong / weak** chemical bonds between the **negative / positive** sodium ions and the **negative / positive** chloride ions. This means that it needs a **little / large** amount of energy to break the bonds.

b) Name two other **properties** of compounds with **ionic structures**.

1. ....

2. ....

Identifying Positive Ions

Q1 Les had four samples of **metal compounds**. He tested each one by placing a small amount on the end of a wire and putting it into a Bunsen flame.

Suggest why putting each of the metal compounds into the flame will allow Les to identify each of the compounds.

....

....

Use the table below to help you answer **Q2** and **Q3**.

Ion	Result of adding NaOH
calcium, Ca^{2+}	white precipitate
copper, Cu^{2+}	light blue precipitate
iron(II), Fe^{2+}	green precipitate
iron(III), Fe^{3+}	red-brown precipitate
zinc, Zn^{2+}	white precipitate (soluble in excess, giving a colourless solution)

You'll be given a table a bit like this in your exam.

Q2 Cilla adds a few drops of **NaOH** solution to solutions of different **metal compounds**.

a) Complete the balanced ionic equation for the reaction of iron(II) ions with hydroxide ions.

Fe^{2+}(..........) + ... OH^-(aq) → .... (s)

b) Write a balanced ionic equation for the reaction of **iron(III) ions** with hydroxide ions.

....

Don't forget state symbols.

c) Cilla adds a few drops of sodium hydroxide solution to **zinc sulfate solution**. Then she continues adding sodium hydroxide to excess. What would she observe at each stage?

....

....

Q3 Select compounds from the box to match the following statements.

KCl	LiCl	$FeSO_4$	NH_4Cl	$FeCl_3$	$ZnSO_4$	NaCl	$CuSO_4$	$CaCl_2$	$MgCl_2$	$BaCl_2$

a) This compound forms a blue precipitate with sodium hydroxide solution. ....

b) This compound forms a white precipitate with sodium hydroxide that dissolves if excess sodium hydroxide is added. ....

c) This compound forms a green precipitate with sodium hydroxide solution. ....

d) This compound forms a reddish brown precipitate with sodium hydroxide solution. ....

Top Tips: You'll be given the table of ion tests in your exam, but you still need to practise using it. Otherwise you'll be in the exam staring at a question about a coloured precipitate being formed when NaOH is added, and you won't be able to find the answer. So make sure you've got the hang of it now.

Identifying Negative Ions

Q1   Give the chemical formulae of the **negative ions** present in the following compounds.

    a)   barium sulfate ....   **b)**   potassium iodide ....   **c)**   silver bromide ....

Use the table below to help you answer **Q2** and **Q3**.

Ion	Test and Result
carbonate, CO_3^{2-}	add dilute acid — carbon dioxide gas produced
chloride, Cl^-	acidify with dilute nitric acid, then add silver nitrate solution — white precipitate
bromide, Br^-	acidify with dilute nitric acid, then add silver nitrate solution — cream precipitate
iodide, I^-	acidify with dilute nitric acid, then add silver nitrate solution — yellow precipitate
sulfate, SO_4^{2-}	acidify, then add barium chloride solution or barium nitrate solution — white precipitate

You'll be given a table a bit like this in your exam.

Q2   Complete the passage below on testing for carbonates.

> A test for the presence of carbonates in an unidentified substance involves
>
> reacting it with dilute .... If carbonates are present
>
> then .... will be formed. You can test for this by
>
> bubbling it through .... to see if it becomes milky.

Q3   Deirdre is testing a set of solutions for **negative ions**. Her results are shown in the table below. Compete the table by identifying the negative ion in each solution.

	Test	Result	Ion
Solution 1	added dilute nitric acid, then silver nitrate	got a cream precipitate	
Solution 2	added dilute nitric acid, then silver nitrate	nothing happened	
	added dilute hydrochloric acid, then barium nitrate	got a white precipitate	
Solution 3	added dilute hydrochloric acid	gas released turned limewater cloudy	

Q4   Complete the following symbol equations for reactions involved in **tests for negative ions**.

    a) $Ag^+(aq) + ... \rightarrow AgCl(s)$

    b) $2HCl(aq) + Na_2CO_3(s) \rightarrow 2NaCl(aq) + ...(l) + ...(g)$

    c) $............... + ... \rightarrow BaSO_4(s)$

You're being a bit negative today, aren't you?

No...

Module C5 — Chemicals of the Natural Environment

Chemicals in the Lithosphere

Q1 Circle the correct words to complete the following paragraph.

> Giant covalent structures contain **charged ions** / **uncharged atoms**. The covalent bonds between the atoms are **strong** / **weak**. Giant covalent structures have **high** / **low** melting points and they are usually **soluble** / **insoluble** in water.

Q2 **Graphite** and **diamond** are both minerals made entirely of **carbon**, but have different **properties**.

   a) Explain why graphite is a good conductor of electricity.

....

....

....

   b) Explain how diamond's structure makes it hard.

....

....

....

Q3 The tables below show the **percentage composition** of samples of two different types of **rock**.

The main constituent of **limestone** is calcium carbonate and the main constituent of **sandstone** is silicon dioxide. Decide which sample is limestone and which sample is sandstone, and explain your answers.

Sample A	% composition
Si	44.0
O	51.0
Al	0.8
Ca	0.7
Mg	0.1
Other	3.4

Sample B	% composition
Si	1.3
O	47.1
Al	1.6
Ca	38.5
C	11.0
Mg	0.5

Sample A is: ....

Reason: ....

Sample B is: ....

Reason: ....

Chemicals in the Lithosphere

Q4 Choose from the words in the box to complete the passage describing the Earth's **lithosphere**.

minerals   aluminium   mantle   silicon
atoms   argon   crust   oxygen

The .... and the part of the .... just below it make

up the Earth's lithosphere. It mostly consists of a mixture of ....

The elements ...., ... and ....

are found in large amounts in the crust.

Q5 The different **forms** of carbon have different **properties** and **uses**.

Match each of these two **uses** to one of the forms of carbon given below,
and explain what **property** each form has that makes it suitable for that use.

glass-cutting tool   pencils

a) **Graphite** Use: ....

Property: ....

....

b) **Diamond** Use: ....

Property: ....

....

Q6 Grains of **sand** are giant covalent structures.

a) What is the chemical name for sand?

....

b) Which two elements does it contain?

.... and ....

c) Give **two chemical properties** of sand and explain each in terms of its structure.

Property 1: ....

....

Property 2: ....

....

Module C5 — Chemicals of the Natural Environment

Metals from Minerals

Q1   Tick the boxes to say if each of the statements below about **metal ores** is **true** or **false**.

True False

a)   Ores are rocks containing minerals from which metals can be extracted.   ☐ ☐

b)   The more reactive the metal, the easier it is to extract from its ore.   ☐ ☐

c)   Zinc, iron and copper can all be extracted by heating their ores with carbon.   ☐ ☐

d)   When a metal oxide loses oxygen, it is reduced.   ☐ ☐

Q2   **Copper** may have first been extracted when someone accidentally dropped copper ore into a **wood fire**. When the ashes were cleared away some copper was left.

a)   Explain how dropping copper ore into a fire could lead to the extraction of copper.

....

....

*Hint: wood contains **carbon**.*

b)   Today large amounts of copper ore are mined to produce copper metal.
Give one reason why so much ore needs to be mined to produce the copper.

....

Q3   Fill in the blanks in the passage below about **extracting metals** from their **ores**.

oxidised	below	carbon	reduced	above	more	electrolysis	neutralisation

.... is often used to extract metals that are .... it in

the reactivity series. It takes the oxygen from a metal oxide, so it is ....

and the metal oxide is .... Other metals have to be extracted using

.... because they are .... reactive.

Q4   Complete the word and symbol equations for the extraction of each of these metals using carbon.

a)   iron oxide + carbon → .... + ...

b)   .... + ... → copper + carbon dioxide

c)   .... + 3CO(g) → 2Fe(s) + 3CO$_2$(g)

d)   2ZnO(s) + ... → .... + CO$_2$(g)

Don't forget the state symbols...

Top Tips: Metals aren't usually found in the ground as pure lumps. They need to be extracted from their ores, and this is done by a variety of methods. The ones you need to know about are reduction using carbon and electrolysis. Which is what these pages are all about...

Electrolysis

Q1 Complete the passage about **electrolysis** using words from the box below.

dissolved	molecules	electric	given to	electrolyte
decompose	external circuit		taken from	molten

During the electrolysis of an ionic compound, an .... current is passed

through a .... or .... ionic substance, causing it

to .... This liquid is called the .... Electrons

are .... ions at the positive electrode and are passed through the

.... to the negative electrode, where they are ....

other ions in the solution. Atoms or .... are formed.

Q2 The diagram below shows the electrolysis of **molten aluminium oxide**.

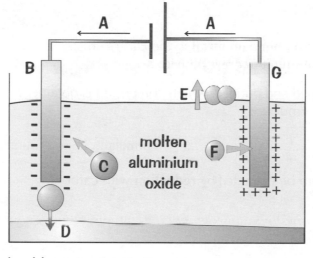 

Write the labels that should go at points A–G:

A ....

B ....

C ....

D ....

E ....

F ....

G ....

Q3 Explain why the **electrolyte** needs to be either a **solution** or **molten** for electrolysis to work.

....

....

Electrolysis

Q4 a) Tick the correct boxes to show whether the following statements are **true** or **false**.

	True	False

i) Ionic substances can only be electrolysed if molten or in solution.

ii) When an ionic solid melts the ions are free to move and carry charge.

iii) During electrolysis, non-metals are attracted to the negative electrode.

iv) In the extraction of aluminium the electrolyte is molten aluminium metal.

v) The aluminium metal produced is molten.

vi) Aluminium ions gain electrons in electrolysis.

b) Write out a correct version of each false statement.

....

....

....

....

Q5 **Aluminium** is the most **abundant** metal in the Earth's crust. The most common aluminium ore is bauxite .

Goodness, how awfully common... °₀₀

a) When this ore is mined and purified, which compound is obtained? Give its name and formula.

Name .... **Formula** ....

b) Why can't aluminium be extracted by **reduction** with carbon?

....

Q6 **Aluminium** is extracted from its ore by **elcctrolysis**.

a) State whether the pure aluminium is formed at the positive or the negative electrode.

....

b) Write balanced half-equations for the reactions at the electrodes.

Negative electrode: ....

Positive electrode: ....

Top Tips: Usually, things that are common are cheap to buy — like potatoes. But, even though aluminium is as common a metal as you're going to get, it's not actually that cheap because it costs a lot to extract. (Potatoes, on the other hand, are easy to extract — just get digging.)

Calculating Masses

Q1   All elements have a relative atomic mass, A_r.

a)   Complete the following sentence by filling in the blanks.

> The relative atomic mass of an element shows the .... of its
>
> atoms relative to the mass of one .... of ....

b)   Give the **relative atomic masses** (A_r) of the following elements. Use the periodic table to help you.

i) magnesium ....   iv) hydrogen ....   vii) K ....

ii) neon ....   v)   C ....   viii) Ca ....

iii) oxygen ....   vi) Cu ....   ix)   Cl ....

Q2 a)   Explain how the **relative formula mass** of a **compound** is calculated.

....

b)   Give the **relative formula masses** (M_r) of the following:

i) water, H_2O ....

ii) potassium chloride, KOH ....

iii) nitric acid, HNO_3 ....

iv) magnesium hydroxide, $Mg(OH)_2$ ....

v) iron(III) hydroxide, $Fe(OH)_3$ ....

Q3   Dave is **calculating** how much **metal** can be **extracted** from certain ores.

a)   Iron can be extracted from its ore in the following reaction:

$$Fe_2O_3 (s) + 3CO(g) \rightarrow 2Fe(s) + 3CO_2(g)$$

Calculate the mass of iron that can be extracted from 500 g iron oxide.

....

....

b)   Could more metal be obtained from the same mass of copper oxide (CuO)?

....

....

Metals

Q1 The table shows the **properties** of **four elements** found in the periodic table.

ELEMENT	MELTING POINT (°C)	DENSITY (g/cm³)	ELECTRICAL CONDUCTIVITY
A	1084	8.9	Excellent
B	−39	13.6	Very good
C	3500	3.51	Very poor
D	1536	7.87	Very good

a) Which **three** of the above elements are most likely to be **metals**?

....

b) Explain how you know the other element is **not** a metal.

....

....

Q2 This table shows some of the **properties** of four different **metals**.

Metal	Heat Conduction	Cost	Electrical Conductivity	Strength
1	average	high	good	good
2	average	medium	good	excellent
3	excellent	low	excellent	good
4	low	high	average	poor

Some metal is heavy.

Use the information in the table to choose which metal would be **best** for making:

a) Saucepan bases ....

b) Car bodies ....

c) Electrical wiring ....

Q3 Complete the following sentences about metals.

a) Metals have a .... structure that is held together by strong bonds.

b) Metals are good conductors of .... and ....

c) The atoms in metals can slide over each other, so metals are ....

Metals

Q4 All metals have a similar **structure**. This explains why many of them have similar **properties**.

a) Draw a labelled diagram of a typical metal structure, showing the electrons.

b) What is unusual about the electrons in a metal?

....

Q5 Complete the following sentences by choosing from the words in the box.

Each word should only be used once (or not at all).

| hammered | weak | low | high | strong | malleable |

a) Metals have a .... tensile strength.

b) Metals are .... and hard to break.

c) Metals can be .... into different shapes because they are ....

Q6 Explain how **electricity** is conducted through metals.

....

....

Q7 Explain why most metals have **high melting points**.

....

....

....

Top Tips: Okay, so metals form weird bonds. The electrons can go wandering about through the material, and it's this that gives them some of their characteristic properties. It's pretty important that you learn the key phrases that examiners like — 'giant structure', 'sea of free electrons', etc.

Module C5 — Chemicals of the Natural Environment

Environmental Impact

Q1 Ores are **finite resources**.

a) Explain what finite resources are.

....

....

b) Explain why it is a **problem** that ores are finite resources.
Suggest one thing that can be done to **reduce** this problem.

....

....

Q2 New **mines** always have **social**, **economic** and **environmental** consequences. Complete this table by putting **two** more effects that a new mine can have in each of the columns.

Remember to include both positive and negative effects.

Social	Economic	Environmental
Services, e.g. Healthcare may be improved because of the influx of people		Pollution from traffic.

Q3 Below is some information about **aluminium**, a widely used metal.

Bauxite mines are often located in rainforests.
Extracting aluminium from bauxite requires huge quantities of electricity.

Briefly describe the environmental consequences of:

a) mining bauxite ....

....

b) extracting aluminium from bauxite ....

....

c) **not** recycling aluminium cans ....

....

Module C5 — Chemicals of the Natural Environment

Mixed Questions — Module C5

Q1 Carbon is found in both **small molecular substances** and **large covalent structures**.

a) Explain why small molecular substances like carbon dioxide have low melting and boiling points.

....

b) Explain why large covalent structures like diamond have high melting and boiling points.

....

Q2 Calcium carbonate is an **ionic compound**.

Look back at the tables on pages 58 and 59 for the tests for ions to help with this question.

a) The charge on a calcium ion is 2+ and the charge on a carbonate ion is 2-. State the formula of calcium carbonate.

....

b) A solution of calcium carbonate was tested for positive and negative ions.

i) Describe what you would expect to see when NaOH was added to the solution.

....

ii) Complete the ionic equation for this reaction. $Ca^{2+}(aq) + 2OH^-(aq) \rightarrow$ ....

iii) Describe what you would expect to see if dilute acid was added to the solution.

....

Q3 **Aluminium** is a very useful metal that is extracted from bauxite ore (Al_2O_3) by electrolysis.

a) Explain why aluminium needs to be extracted using electrolysis.

....

b) Write a balanced symbol equation for the decomposition of Al_2O_3 into aluminium and oxygen.

....

c) Calculate how much aluminium could be extracted from 600 g of bauxite ore.

....

....

d) Aluminium is often used to make panels for cars. Suggest **two** properties of aluminium that make it suitable for this purpose.

....

Industrial Chemical Synthesis

Q1   Explain what is meant by **chemical synthesis**.

....

....

Q2   Tick the boxes to show whether the following are usually produced on a **small** or **large scale**.

	Small scale	Large scale
a) Pharmaceuticals	✓	☐
b) Sulfuric acid (H_2SO_4)	☐	✓
c) Fertiliser	✓	☐

Q3   Modern industries uses huge amounts of **sulfuric acid** every day. The chart below shows how sulfuric acid produced by one particular chemical plant is **used**.

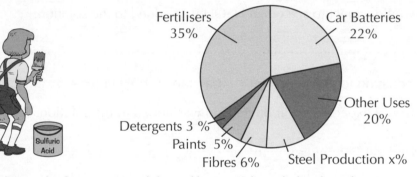

Fertilisers 35%
Car Batteries 22%
Other Uses 20%
Detergents 3 %
Paints 5%
Fibres 6%
Steel Production x%

a)   What is the **largest use** of the sulfuric acid made by this plant?

Fertilisers

....

b)   What percentage of the sulfuric acid from this plant is used in the production of steel?

9 %

....

Q4   The bar chart shows the number of people **employed** in various sectors of the **chemical industry** in country X.

a)   Which **sector** employs the **most** people?

Pharmaceuticals

....

b)   How many people **in total** are employed in the chemical industry in country X?

18,000

....

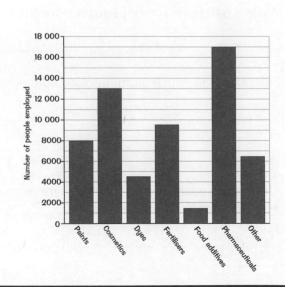

Acids and Alkalis

Q1   Complete each of the following sentences with a single word.

a)   Solutions which are not acidic or alkaline are said to be .... *neutral* ....

b)   A neutral substance has a pH of .... *7* ....

c)   Universal indicator is a combination of different ....

d)   An alkali is a substance with a pH that is .... *higher* .... than 7.

e)   Litmus paper turns .... *blue.* .... when a solution is alkaline.

Q2   Draw lines to match the substances and their universal indicator colours to their **pH** values and **acid/alkali strengths**.

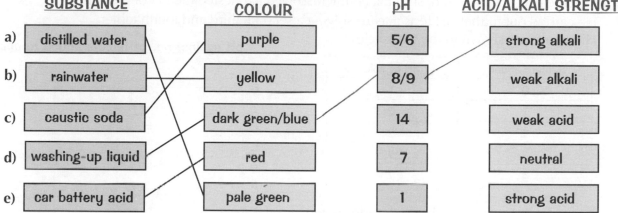

SUBSTANCE	UNIVERSAL INDICATOR COLOUR	pH	ACID/ALKALI STRENGTH
a) distilled water	purple	5/6	strong alkali
b) rainwater	yellow	8/9	weak alkali
c) caustic soda	dark green/blue	14	weak acid
d) washing-up liquid	red	7	neutral
e) car battery acid	pale green	1	strong acid

Q3   Many chemicals that people use **every day** are **acids** or **alkalis**.

a)   Complete the following passage using words from the box.

hydrogen chloride   solids   more   tartaric   ethanoic   less   liquid   nitric

Acids are substances with a pH of .... *less* .... than 7.

Pure acidic compounds are found in various different states, for example citric

acid and .... *nitric* .... acid are both .... *liquid* ....

Sulfuric acid is an example of a .... *liquid* .... acidic compound,

as are .... *tartaric* .... and .... *ethanoic* .... acids.

There are also acidic compounds that are gases — .... *hydrogen   chloride*

is one example.

b)   Name three common **alkalis** that are **metal hydroxides**.

.... *sodium hydroxide ,   Pottasium hydroxide ,   magnesium hydroxide*

Acids and Alkalis

Q4 **Indigestion** is caused by **too much acid** in the stomach.
Antacid tablets contain **alkalis**, which neutralise the excess acid.

a) Which is the correct word equation for a **neutralisation reaction**? Circle the correct answer.

salt + acid → alkali + water   (acid + alkali → salt + water)   acid + water → alkali + salt

b) State what ions are produced when:

i) an acidic compound is dissolved in water.

h+

ii) an alkaline compound is dissolved in water.

OH⁻

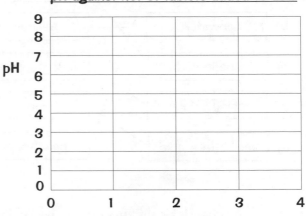

Joey wanted to test whether some antacid tablets really did **neutralise acid**. He added a tablet
to some hydrochloric acid, stirred it until it dissolved and tested the pH of the solution.
He carried out further pH tests after dissolving a second, third and fourth tablet.
His results are shown in the table below.

Tablets added	pH of acid
0	1
1	2
2	3
3	7
4	7

pH against no. of tablets added to acid

c) i) Plot a graph of the results on the grid shown.

ii) How many tablets were
needed to neutralise the acid? ....

d) Give two ways Joey could have tested the pH of the solution.

1. .... litmus   paper ....

2. .... Universal   indicator. ....

Q5 When an acid and an alkali react the products are **neutral**. This is called a **neutralisation** reaction.

a) Describe what happens to the **ions** from the acid and the **ions** from the alkali during a
neutralisation reaction.

They   cancel   out   and   for   water   to   make
H₂O.   making   a   neutral   atom.

b) Write a balanced symbol equation to show the reaction between the **ions**
from the acid and the **ions** from the alkali during a neutralisation reaction.

H⁺ + OH⁻ ⟶ H₂O

Acids Reacting with Metals

Q1   The diagram below shows **magnesium** reacting with **hydrochloric acid**.

a)   Label the diagram with the names of the chemicals.

hydrochloric acid

hydrogen.

magnesium

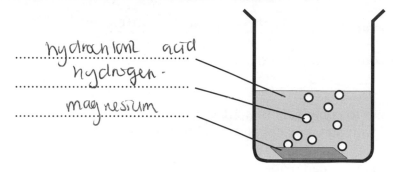

b)   Complete the word equation for this reaction:

magnesium + ...hydrochloric acid...... → **magnesium chloride** + ...hydrogen..........

c)   Write a **balanced** symbol equation for the reaction.

2mg + 2HCL → 2MgCL + H₂

The formula of magnesium chloride is MgCl₂.

d)   All metals will react with acids in a similar way.
Zinc reacts with sulfuric acid. Give the **word** equation for this reaction.

2Z + 2 HSO₄ → 2Z SO₄ + H₂

Q2   Write out **balanced** symbol equations for the following reactions. Include **state symbols**.

a)   calcium + hydrochloric acid

2Ca + 2HCL → 2CaCL + H₂

b)   zinc + hydrochloric acid

2Zn + 2HCL → ZnCL + H₂

c)   magnesium + sulfuric acid

Mg + HSO₄ → Mg SO₄ + H₂

d)   **Hydrobromic acid** reacts with **magnesium** to form a bromide salt and hydrogen.

i)   The unbalanced symbol equation for this reaction is shown below. Balance the equation.

..2.. Mg (s) + ..4.. HBr (aq) → ..2.. MgBr₂ (aq) + ..2.. H₂ (g)

ii)   Write a balanced symbol equation for the reaction between **aluminium** and hydrobromic acid.
(The formula of aluminium bromide is AlBr₃.)

2Al + 6HBr → 2AlBr₃ + 3H₂

Oxides, Hydroxides and Carbonates

Q1 Give the **general word equation** for the reaction between an **acid** and:

a) a metal oxide ...... acid + metal oxide → metal salt + water

b) a metal carbonate ...... acid + metal carbonate → metal salt + water + CO_2

c) a metal hydroxide ...... acid + metal hydroxide → metal salt + water

Q2 Fill in the blanks to complete the word equations for **acids** reacting with **metal oxides** and **metal hydroxides**.

A metal-ox-hide

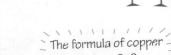

a) hydrochloric acid + lead oxide → ...... lead ...... chloride + water

b) nitric acid + copper hydroxide → copper ...... nitrate ...... + water

c) sulfuric acid + zinc oxide → zinc sulfate + ... water ......

d) hydrochloric acid + ... sodium ...... oxide → sodium ...... chloride ...... + ... water ......

e) ...... nitric ...... acid + copper oxide → ...... copper ...... nitrate + ... water ......

f) nitric acid + ... sodium ...... hydroxide → sodium ...... nitrate ...... + ... water ......

Q3 Complete the following symbol equations for **acids** reacting with **metal carbonates**.

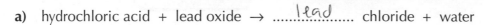

a) $6HNO_{3(aq)}$ $3Na_2CO_{3(s)}$ → ...... $6NaNO_3$ ...... + ... $3H_2O$ ...... + ... $3CO_2$ ......

b) $H_2SO_{4(aq)} +$ ...... $MgCO_3$ ...... → $MgSO_{4(aq)} +$ ...... H_2O ...... + ... CO_2 ......

Q4 Write symbol equations for the following reactions.

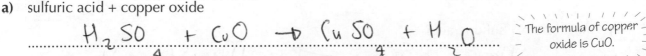

The formula of copper oxide is CuO.

a) sulfuric acid + copper oxide

...... $H_2SO_4 + CuO → CuSO_4 + H_2O$ ......

b) nitric acid + magnesium oxide

...... $H_2NO_3 + Mg_2O → MgNO_3 → H_2O$ ......

c) sulfuric acid + sodium hydroxide

...... $H_2SO_4 + NaOH → Na_2SO_4 + H_2O$ ......

Top Tips: At first glance it looks quite scary, all this writing equations — but it's not that bad, honest. The key is to learn the basic rules inside out. Once you've got them mastered it's really just a case of swapping a few bits round and filling in the gaps. No reason to panic at all.

Oxides, Hydroxides and Carbonates

Q5 Acids react with **metal carbonates** in neutralisation reactions. Write **balanced symbol equations** for the following reactions.

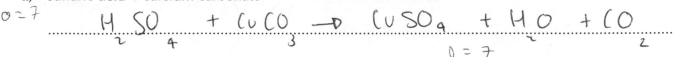

Make sure you include state symbols for all these reactions.

a) sulfuric acid + calcium carbonate

$$O = 7 \quad H_2SO_4 + CuCO_3 \rightarrow CuSO_4 + H_2O + CO_2$$
$$O = 7$$

b) nitric acid + magnesium carbonate

$$H_2NO_3 + MgCO_3 \rightarrow MgNO_3 + H_2O + CO_2$$

c) hydrochloric acid + potassium carbonate

$$2HCL_4 + 2KCO_3 \rightarrow 2KCL + H_2O_2 + 2CO_3$$

d) hydrochloric acid + calcium carbonate

e) sulfuric acid + sodium carbonate

Q6 Amir was investigating how he could restore a tarnished copper ornament. He obtained some **copper compounds** and looked at the effect of reacting them with dilute **hydrochloric acid** (HCl).

SUBSTANCE TESTED	FORMULA	COLOUR	OBSERVATIONS WHEN ADDED TO THE ACID
copper carbonate	$CuCO_3$	green	fizzed and dissolved forming a blue solution
copper hydroxide	$Cu(OH)_2$	blue	dissolved slowly forming a blue solution
copper oxide	CuO	black	dissolved very slowly forming a blue solution

a) **i)** Why does copper carbonate fizz when it reacts with an acid?

ii) Write a word equation for the reaction between hydrochloric acid and copper carbonate.

b) Amir tested part of the copper ornament with the acid and it fizzed. Which compound is likely to be present on the surface of the ornament?

c) Write a balanced symbol equation for the reaction of hydrochloric acid with copper hydroxide.

<u>Synthesising Compounds</u>

Q1 Draw lines to match each description to the type of reaction it is describing.

an acid and an alkali react to produce a salt

a compound breaks down on heating

an insoluble solid forms when two solutions are mixed

precipitation

neutralisation

thermal decomposition

Q2 In the synthesis of any **inorganic chemical** there are a number of **important stages**.

a) Complete the passage using words from the box below.

harmed	reduce	hazards	injury	action

A risk assessment should identify any stage in the process that could cause ......*hazards*...... *injury*

This usually involves identifying ......*hazards*...... and the people who might be

......*harmed*...... Risk assessments also include what ......*action*...... can be taken

to ......*reduce*...... the risk.

b) When making a chemical on an industrial scale it is often important to calculate accurately the quantities of reactants to be used. Explain why.

......so none is waste or waste is......

......minimized.......

c) Give **two** factors that should be considered when choosing the apparatus in which a reaction will be carried out.

......the right size......

......the right strength.......

d) Give two reaction conditions that need to be considered when designing a synthesis reaction.

......temperature , concentration.......

Q3 Explain why each of the following might be carried out during chemical synthesis.

a) Crystallisation

......purifies sample by forming crystals from cooled solution......

b) Evaporation

......remove excess solvent from solution.......

c) Drying

......remove excess water w/ out removing yield.......

Synthesising Compounds

Q4 Read the article below and answer the questions that follow.

Sodium Bromide

To most people sodium bromide looks like any other white, crystalline salt. What they don't realise is the vast number of uses it has in the chemical industry, ranging from photography to pharmaceuticals. As with most inorganic chemicals, there are a number of different stages in the production of sodium bromide.

Industrial Synthesis

Sodium bromide (NaBr) is usually produced by reacting sodium hydroxide (NaOH) with hydrobromic acid (HBr):

Sodium hydroxide + hydrobromic acid › sodium bromide + water

After reacting sodium hydroxide with hydrobromic acid, the sodium bromide is extracted by evaporation — this involves heating the sodium bromide solution. The water is evaporated, leaving behind white crystals of sodium bromide. After the product has been isolated it is then purified.

Yield and purity

The yield of sodium bromide produced is then calculated. For financial reasons it's important to produce a high yield, so chemical engineers are always looking for ways to modify the process to give a higher yield. The purity of the product is also calculated at this stage.

a) i) What type of reaction is used to produce sodium bromide?

neutralisation

  ii) Write a balanced symbol equation (including state symbols) to show the formation of sodium bromide.

$3NaOH + 3HBr \rightarrow 3NaBr + 3H_2O$

b) Sodium bromide is a soluble compound.
Name a method you could use to separate an **insoluble** product from the reaction mixture.

c) Why is it useful to calculate the **yield** of sodium bromide?

d) Suggest a method that could be used to **purify** the sodium bromide.

crystallisation.

Calculating Masses in Reactions

Q1 Anna burns **10 g** of **magnesium** in air to produce **magnesium oxide** (MgO).

a) Write out the **balanced equation** for this reaction.

$$Mg + O_2 \longrightarrow 2MgO$$

magnesium + oxygen

b) Calculate the mass of **magnesium oxide** that's produced.

$$2MgO \longrightarrow \quad Mg = 24 \times 2 = 48$$
$$O = 16 \times 2 = 32 \quad + \quad = \quad 80$$
$$\overline{80g}$$

Q2 What mass of **sodium** is needed to make **2 g** of **sodium oxide**?

$$4Na + O_2 \rightarrow 2Na_2O$$

Q3 **Aluminium** and **iron oxide** (Fe_2O_3) react together to produce **aluminium oxide** (Al_2O_3) and **iron**.

a) Write out the **balanced equation** for this reaction.

b) What **mass** of iron is produced from **20 g** of iron oxide?

Q4 When heated, **limestone** ($CaCO_3$) decomposes to form **calcium oxide** (CaO) and **carbon dioxide**.

How many **kilograms** of limestone are needed to make **100 kilograms** of **calcium oxide**?

The calculation is exactly the same — just use 'kg' instead of 'g'.

Top Tips: The periodic table really comes in useful here. There's no way you'll be able to answer these questions without one (unless you've memorised all the elements' relative atomic masses — and that would just be silly). And luckily for you, you'll be given one in your exam too. Yay!

Calculating Masses in Reactions

Q5 **Iron oxide** is reduced to **iron** inside a blast furnace using carbon. There are **three** stages involved.

Stage A	$C + O_2 \rightarrow CO_2$
Stage B	$CO_2 + C \rightarrow 2CO$
Stage C	$3CO + Fe_2O_3 \rightarrow 2Fe + 3CO_2$

If **10 g** of **carbon** are used in stage B, and all the carbon monoxide produced gets used in stage C, what **mass** of CO_2 is produced in **stage C**?

Work out the mass of CO at the end of stage B first.

....

....

....

....

....

Q6 **Sodium sulfate** (Na_2SO_4) is made by reacting **sodium hydroxide** (NaOH) with **sulfuric acid** (H_2SO_4). **Water** is also produced.

a) Write out the **balanced equation** for this reaction.

....

b) What mass of **sodium hydroxide** is needed to make **75 g** of **sodium sulfate**?

....

....

....

....

c) What mass of **water** is formed when **50 g** of **sulfuric acid** reacts?

....

....

....

....

Purification and Measuring Yield

Q1 James wanted to produce **silver chloride** (AgCl). He added a carefully measured mass of silver nitrate to some dilute hydrochloric acid. An **insoluble white solid** formed.

a) Complete the formula for calculating percentage yield, and its labels, using words from the box. Words can be used more than once.

| reactants weighing theoretical yield pure dried actual yield maximum |

This is the mass of pure dry product. It is found by

.... the dried product.

percentage yield = $\dfrac{\text{..}}{\text{..}} \times 100$

This is the ....

of the product as a percentage of the

....

This is the .... amount of

.................................., dried product that

could have been made using the amounts of

.... you started with.

b) James calculated that he should get 2.7 g of silver chloride, but he only got 1.2 g. What was the **percentage yield**?

....

c) What **method** should James use to separate the silver chloride from the solution?

....

d) James left the silver chloride to dry on the bench. Suggest two ways the product could have been dried if the reaction was being carried out on a large scale.

1. ....

2. ....

Q2 Explain how you could separate a **soluble solid** from a solution.

....

....

Titrations

Q1 **Titrations** are used widely in industry, for example when determining the **purity** of a substance.

a) If a solid product is being tested why must it first be made into a **solution**?

titration only work with solutions.

b) Fill in the blanks using words from the box below to describe how a solution is made and draw lines to connect each statement to the diagram it describes.
You can use the words more than once.

| solvent | weigh | swirl | dissolved | crush | water |

① ....*crush*.......... the solid product into a powder.

② .....*weigh*........ some of the powdered product into a titration flask.

③ The powder is then .....*dissolved*..... by adding some ......*solvent*...... (e.g. ......*water*.........).

④ ....*swirl*........ the flask until all of the solid has ....*dissolved*

c) Label the following pieces of apparatus used in a titration experiment.

burrette

titration flask.

d) Describe how you would carry out an acid-alkali titration.

Pour acid into titration flask. Mix in some Universal indicator. Put some alkali into burette. Slowly put acid into solution. When end point is near, slow down. When colour changes, note down amount of alkali used.

Talk about tight rations

Module C6 — Chemical Synthesis

Purity

Q1　**Pharmaceutical companies** need to ensure that the drugs they produce are **pure**.

a)　Give two methods that can be used to improve the purity of a product.

1. ....　　2. ....

b)　Why is it important to control the purity of chemicals such as pharmaceuticals?

They make drugs that are consumed by humans.
Impurities can harm humans.

Q2　Ruth works in the quality assurance department of a company that produces **fizzy drinks**. The drinks contain **citric acid**. One of Ruth's jobs is to test the **purity** of the citric acid before it is used to make the drinks. She does this by carrying out an acid-alkali **titration**.

a)　What type of reaction do titrations involve? Circle the correct answer.

precipitation　　　　esterification　　　　(neutralisation)

b)　Ruth starts off with **0.3 g of impure citric acid** dissolved in **25 cm³** of water. When she carries out the titration she finds that it takes **21.6 cm³ of 2.5 g/dm³ sodium hydroxide** (NaOH) to neutralise the citric acid. Calculate the purity of the citric acid by completing the following steps.

i)　Calculate the **concentration** of the citric acid solution in g/dm³ using the equation:

$$\text{conc. of citric acid solution} = 4.8 \times \frac{\text{conc. of NaOH} \times \text{vol. of NaOH}}{\text{vol. of citric acid solution}}$$

To get from cm³ to dm³ you divide by 1000.

....

....

....

ii)　Calculate the **mass** of the citric acid in g using the equation:

$$\text{mass of citric acid} = \text{concentration of citric acid} \times \text{volume}$$

....

iii)　Calculate the **percentage purity** of the citric acid using the equation:

$$\% \text{ purity} = \frac{\text{calculated mass of citric acid}}{\text{mass of impure citric acid at start}} \times 100\%$$

....

....

Energy Transfer in Reactions

Q1 Use the words below to **complete** the blanks in the passage.
You can use the words more than once.

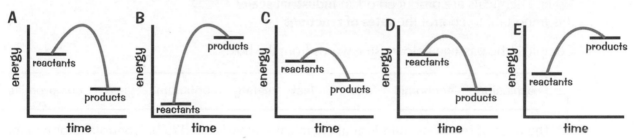

endothermic   exothermic   energy   heat   an increase   a decrease

All chemical reactions involve changes in ....

In .... reactions, ... energy is given out to the

surroundings. A thermometer will show .... in temperature.

In .... reactions, ... energy is taken in from the

surroundings. A thermometer will show .... in temperature.

Q2 **Energy level diagrams** can be used to show whether a reaction is exothermic or endothermic.

A — energy/time, reactants, products
B — energy/time, products, reactants
C — energy/time, reactants, products
D — energy/time, reactants, products
E — energy/time, products, reactants

Which diagram(s) show:

a) an exothermic reaction? ....

b) an endothermic reaction? ....

Q3 Miranda is trying to synthesise **two** different chemicals. One of the
synthesis reactions is **exothermic** and one is **endothermic**.

a) She carries out the **exothermic** reaction in a container surrounded by ice.
Explain why Miranda does this.

....

....

b) She carries out the **endothermic** reaction in a container placed on a hot plate.
Explain why Miranda does this.

....

....

Top Tips: This stuff isn't as bad as it seems — honest. You've just gotta remember that
energy is released in exothermic reactions (like fires and explosions) and **energy is taken in** in
endothermic reactions (like thermal decomposition reactions). This energy is usually in the form of **heat**.

Rates of Reaction

Q1 Chemical reactions occur at different **rates**.

a) Draw a line to match these common chemical reactions to the **speed** at which they happen.

| a firework exploding | SLOW (hours or longer) | a match burning |

| hair being dyed | MODERATE SPEED (minutes) | a ship rusting |

| an apple rotting | FAST (seconds or shorter) |

b) Explain what is meant by the term 'rate of chemical reaction'.

....

....

Q2 When chemicals are produced on an **industrial scale** it is important to control the **rates of reactions**.

Complete the passage below using words from the box.

| explosion economic costs fast safety optimum yield compromise |

The rates of reactions in industrial chemical synthesis need to be controlled for two main

reasons. Firstly for .... reasons. If the reaction is too

.... it could cause an ...., which may injure or

even kill employees. Chemical reactions are also controlled for ....

reasons. Companies usually choose .... conditions. These will often

involve a .... between the ...., rate of reaction

and production ....

Q3 The graph shows the results from an experiment using **magnesium** and dilute **hydrochloric acid**. The **volume of gas** produced was measured at regular intervals as the reaction proceeded.

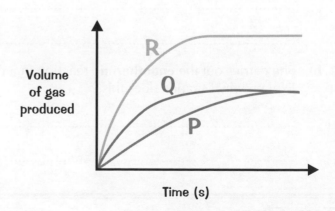

a) Which reaction was **faster**, P or Q?

....

b) Which reaction produced the **largest volume of gas**, P, Q or R?

....

c) On the curve for reaction R, mark with an **X** the point where the reaction finishes.

Rates of Reaction

Q4 You can control the rate of a reaction by changing the **conditions**.

a) Suggest why you might want to use a very **high temperature** for a reaction.

....

....

b) Give **two** reasons why you might use a **low temperature** instead.

Nora's reactions were slow in the cold.

1. ....

2. ....

Q5 In an experiment to investigate **reaction rates**, strips of **magnesium** were put into tubes containing different concentrations of **hydrochloric acid**. The time taken for the magnesium to 'disappear' was measured. The results are shown in the table.

Conc. of acid (mol/dm^3)	Time taken (seconds)
0.01	298
0.02	147
0.04	74
0.08	37
0.10	30
0.20	15

a) Give **three** things that should be kept the same in each case to make this a **fair test**.

....

....

b) Plot a graph of the data on the grid provided, with concentration of acid on the horizontal axis and time on the vertical axis.

c) What do the results tell you about how the concentration of acid affects the rate of the reaction?

....

d) Would the rates of the reaction have been different if magnesium powder had been used instead? If so, how?

....

....

Collision Theory

Q1   Complete the following passage by circling the correct word(s) from each pair.

> In order for a reaction to occur, the particles must **remain still** / **collide**.
>
> Anything that makes particles collide **more often** / **less often** or with
>
> **more energy** / **less energy** will increase the rate of reaction. For example,
>
> increasing the temperature increases the **concentration** / **rate of reaction**.

Q2   Reactions involving solutions are affected by the **concentration**.

a)   If you increase the concentration of a solution, does the rate of reaction **increase** or **decrease**?
Explain your answer.

....

....

b)   In the boxes on the right, draw:
  • a diagram showing a **solution** containing two
    different types of particle at **low concentration**
  • a diagram showing a **high concentration** of the same solution.

  ⌐ Think about the number of particles ⌐
  ⌐ there will be at each concentration. ⌐

  low   high
  concentration   concentration

Q3   Here are five statements about **surface area** and rates of reaction.
Tick the appropriate box to show whether each is **true** or **false**.

                                                                                    True False

a)   Breaking a solid into smaller pieces decreases its surface area.   ☐   ☐

b)   A larger surface area will mean a faster rate of reaction.   ☐   ☐

c)   A larger surface area decreases the number of useful collisions.   ☐   ☐

d)   Powdered marble has a larger surface area than the same mass of marble chips. ☐ ☐

e)   A powdered solid reactant produces more product overall than an   ☐   ☐
equal mass of reactant in large lumps does.

Q4   Some reactions use **catalysts**. What is a catalyst?

....

....

Top Tips: It's a pretty good idea to learn the four things that reaction rate depends on
(temperature, concentration, surface area and using a catalyst). It's an even better idea to learn
exactly how these four things affect the rate of a reaction and what happens when you change them.

Module C6 — Chemical Synthesis

Measuring Rates of Reaction

Q1   Complete the following sentence by circling the correct word from each pair.

> The **speed** / **volume** of a reaction can be measured by observing either how quickly the
>
> **products** / **reactants** are used up or how quickly the **products** / **reactants** are formed.

Q2   Charlie was comparing the rate of reaction of 5 g of magnesium ribbon with 20 ml
of **five different concentrations** of hydrochloric acid. Each time he measured the
volume of **gas** that was produced during the **first minute** of the reaction.

a)   In the space below draw the apparatus that Charlie could use to measure the **volume** of
gas produced.

b)   Describe what Charlie could do if he wanted to follow the rate of reaction by calculating the
change in **mass** over the course of the reaction.

....

....

....

Q3   Horatio was investigating the reaction between **lead nitrate** and different
concentrations of **hydrochloric acid**. When lead nitrate and hydrochloric
acid react they produce **lead chloride**, which is an **insoluble solid**.

a)   What name is given to this type of reaction?

....

acid concentration

b)   Describe how Horatio could measure the rate of reaction.

....

....

....

Mixed Questions — Module C6

Q1   Harold is trying to make **magnesium chloride** by reacting
hydrochloric acid with magnesium hydroxide.

a)   He uses a dilute solution of hydrochloric acid with **pH 2**.
What colour would the solution go if universal indicator was added to it?

....

b) i)   Write a balanced symbol equation (including state symbols) for the
reaction between **hydrochloric acid** and **magnesium hydroxide**.

....

ii) What type of reaction is this?

....

c) i)   During the reaction Harold notices that the reaction flask heats up. Explain why this happens.

....

ii) Circle the energy level diagram which best shows the energy levels
of the reactants and products in this reaction.

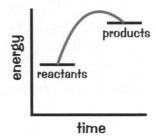
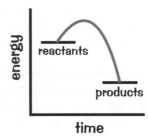

iii) What could Harold do to ensure the reaction is **controlled**?

....

d)   The product of the reaction ($MgCl_2$) is highly **soluble**.

i)   Name a method Harold could use to separate the product from the reaction mixture.

....

ii) Harold wants to improve the purity of the product by using recrystallisation.
Briefly describe how he could do this.

....

iii) Harold calculated that he should get 4.2 g of $MgCl_2$ from the reaction. He only gets 3.2 g.
Calculate the percentage yield of the reaction.

....

....

Speed

Q1   I rode my bike **1500 m** to the shops. It took me **5 minutes**.

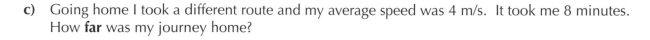

a)   What was my average **speed** in **m/s**?

Remember to convert the times given into the right <u>units</u>.

....

b)   One part of the journey was downhill and I averaged 15 m/s over this 300 m stretch. How **long** did it take to cover this bit of the journey?

....

c)   Going home I took a different route and my average speed was 4 m/s. It took me 8 minutes. How **far** was my journey home?

....

Q2   Paolo and some friends want to order a **takeaway**. Paolo writes down what they know about the two nearest takeaways:

<u>Ludo's Pizza</u>	<u>Moonlight Indian Takeaway</u>
• Time taken to cook the food is 1/4 hour	• Time taken to cook the food is 1/2 hour
• Distance to the house is 6.5 km	• Distance to the house is 4 km
• Deliver on scooters with average speed of 30 km/h	• Delivery van has average speed of 40 km/h

Remember to add on the time taken to cook the food.

Which takeaway should they order from to get their food the **quickest**?

....

....

Q3   **Speed cameras** can be used to catch speeding motorists. The section of road in the diagram below has a **speed limit** of **50 miles per hour**.

a)   1 mile = 1609 metres. Show that 50 miles per hour is about the same speed as **22 m/s**.

....

b)   The diagram below shows a car passing in front of a speed camera. The two pictures show the position of the car **0.2 s** apart. The distance between each white line on the road is **2 m**.

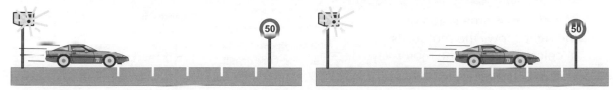

Was the car breaking the speed limit? Show your working.

....

....

Speed, Distance and Velocity

Q1   A **hare** challenges a **tortoise** to a **race**. The hare is so confident he'll win that he takes a nap on the way — but he sleeps for too long and the tortoise wins instead. Here are some facts and figures about the race:

The **tortoise** ran at a constant speed of **5 m/s** throughout the race — pretty impressive.

The **hare** ran at **10 m/s** for **300 s** before falling asleep. He slept for **600 s** and then carried on at **10 m/s** towards the finish line.

The length of the **race track** was **5000 m**.

a)   How far did the hare travel before falling asleep?

....

b)   Add the information about the hare's run to the graph below.

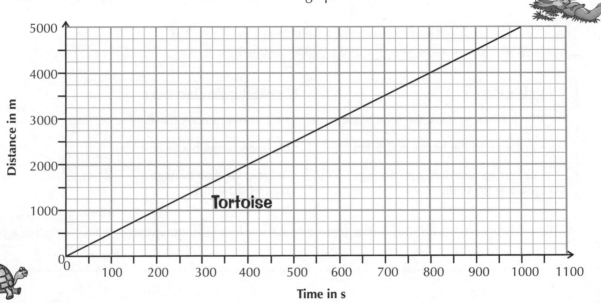

c)   When did the tortoise overtake the hare?

....

d)   How long did the tortoise have to wait at the finish line before the hare arrived?

....

Q2   The speed limit for cars on the **motorway** is **70 mph** (about **31 m/s**). A motorist accelerated onto the motorway from a service station and was captured on a speed camera. He denied speeding.

The **distance-time** graph on the right shows the motorist's acceleration on to the motorway. Was the motorist speeding?

Think... you need to find the speed from a distance-time graph.

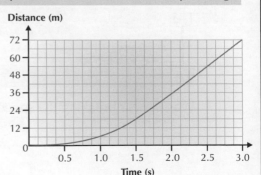

....

....

Speed, Distance and Velocity

Q3 A train travels from A to B and back again. Its speed at each point on the journey A → B is identical to the speed at the equivalent point of the return journey.

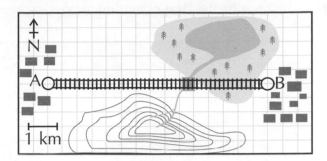

Halfway from A to B, the instantaneous velocity of the train is 15 m/s.

Tick the boxes to show whether the following statements are **true** or **false**.

At the halfway point of the journey B → A:

True False

a) the train's instantaneous speed is 15 m/s. ☐ ☐

b) the train's instantaneous velocity is 15 m/s. ☐ ☐

c) the train's instantaneous velocity is –15 m/s. ☐ ☐

d) the train's average speed is –15 m/s. ☐ ☐

Q4 The graph shows the motion of a **model train**.

a) Describe the motion of the train in the sections marked:

A ....

B ....

C ....

D ....

b) What is the train's speed in section B?

....

....

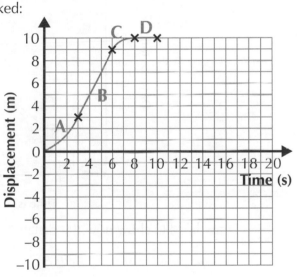

c) Complete the graph for the rest of the train's journey using the following information:

Time	Motion
10 - 12 s	Accelerating backwards (towards the start of the track) for 2 m.
12 - 16 s	Moving at a constant speed of 3 m/s backwards.
16 - 17 s	Decelerating for 1 m
17 - 18 s	Stationary
18 - 19 s	Accelerating for 1 m forwards (towards the start of the track)
19 - 20 s	Moving at a constant speed of 2 m/s forwards.

Top Tips: Remember, speed and velocity are basically the same thing (they're measured in the same way...), it's just that when you talk about velocity you've got to give a direction. As for all those distance-time graphs, they're not too bad once you've practised. Make sure you've got these ones right.

Acceleration and Velocity

Q1   Describe the **type of motion** happening at each of the labelled points on the velocity-time graph.

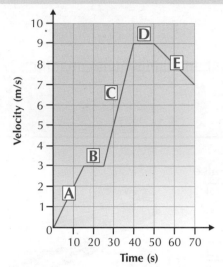

(A) ....

(B) ....

(C) ....

(D) ....

(E) ....

Q2   The distance-time graph and the velocity-time graph below both indicate the **same** three journeys.

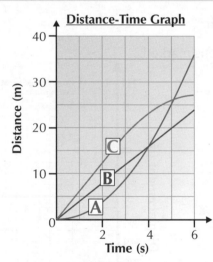

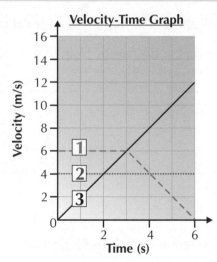

Draw lines to show how the distance-time and velocity-time graphs match up.

Line **A**   Line **1**

Line **B**   Line **2**

Line **C**   Line **3**

Q3   An egg is dropped from the top of the Eiffel tower. It hits the ground after **8 seconds**, at a speed of **80 m/s**.

You'll need to use acceleration = change in velocity ÷ time.

a)   Calculate the egg's acceleration.

....

b)   How long did it take for the egg to reach a velocity of 40 m/s? Assume it falls with a constant acceleration.

....

Acceleration and Velocity

Q4 A car accelerates at **2 m/s²**. After **4 seconds** it reaches a speed of **24 m/s**.

How fast was it going before it started to accelerate?

....

....

....

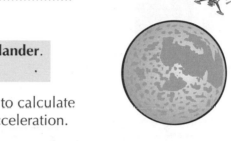

Q5 Below is a **velocity-time** graph for the descent of a **lunar lander**. It accelerates due to the pull of **gravity** from the Moon.

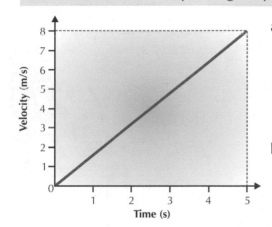

a) Use the graph to calculate the lander's acceleration.

....

....

b) On the same axes, draw the velocity-time graph you would expect if the lander descended on to a planet where the acceleration due to gravity was 1 m/s².

Q6 A motorist saw a **kitten** on the road **25 m** in front of him. It took him **0.75 s** to react and slam on the brakes. His vehicle was initially travelling at **12 m/s** and took **2.5 s** to stop.

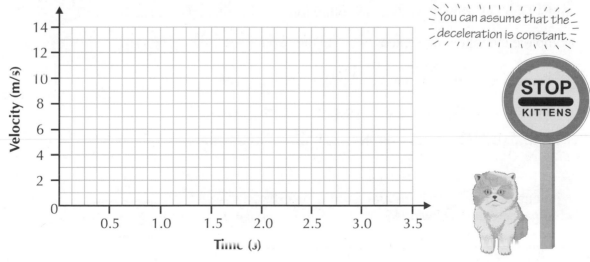

You can assume that the deceleration is constant.

a) Complete the velocity-time graph for the vehicle from the point at which he saw the kitten.

b) Calculate the deceleration of the vehicle between applying the brakes and stopping.

....

....

Forces and Friction

Q1 Complete the following passage.

When an object exerts a ....*force*.............. on another

object, it experiences a force in return. The two forces are

called an ....*interaction*.......... pair. For example, if someone

leans on a wall with a force of 150 N, the wall exerts a force

of ....*150*................. N in the opposite direction — an

'..............................' and ....' reaction.

Q2 On the way down a slide, a penguin experiences **friction**.

a) Between which two surfaces is friction acting?

...........*Penguin   and   slide.*..........

b) On the picture, draw an arrow to show the **direction**
in which friction is acting on the penguin.

c) Suggest how the penguin could **reduce** friction to speed up his slide.

...........*add   lubricant.*..........

Q3 A **flamingo** is standing on one leg. The force, **A**,
is the flamingo pushing down on the ground.

a) Add a labelled arrow B to show the other force in the interaction pair.

b) Complete the following sentences about the two forces:

Force A is exerted by the ....*flam*................ **on**

the ....*ground.*............ **. Force B is exerted by the**

..........*ground*.......... **on the** ......*flam*............ **.**

Q4 A **jet engine** uses air to burn fuel, producing **exhaust** gases
which accelerate **backwards** from the rear of the engine.

exhaust
gases

a) Complete this sentence by circling the correct word(s).

The exhaust gases accelerate because the **air** / (**jet engine**) exerts (**a force** / **friction**) on them.

b) Explain how this process makes a jet aircraft move **forwards**.

....

....

Forces

Q1 A **teapot** sits on a table.

a) Explain why it **doesn't** sink into the table.

The table too exerts a force on teapot. (reaction).

b) Jane picks up the teapot and hangs it from the ceiling by a **rope**. What **vertical** forces now act on the teapot?

lift and gravity (weight).

c) Draw on and label the diagram on the right to show the forces **acting on the teapot** as it hangs.

lift

weight (gravity)

Q2 The diagram below shows the **forces** acting on an **aeroplane**.

lift

drag ← → thrust

weight

The aircraft is flying horizontally at a constant speed of 200 m/s. Which of the following statements about the aeroplane is true? Circle the appropriate letter.

A The thrust is bigger than the drag and the lift is bigger than the weight. ✗

B The thrust is smaller than the drag and the lift is equal to the weight. ✗

C The thrust is equal to the drag and the lift is bigger than the weight.

D The thrust is equal to the drag and the lift is equal to the weight. ✓

Q3 A bear weighing **700 N** rides a bike at a **constant speed** with a driving force of **1500 N**.

a) Label the forces acting on the bear, the air and the ground. Include the size of each force.

reaction

thrust

drag

weight

b) The bear brakes and slows down. Which direction is the resultant force in?

Forces and Momentum

Q1 The **force diagram** on the right shows a **train** pulling out of a station.

Calculate the resultant force acting on the train in the following directions:

a) Vertical: ....0........................

b) Horizontal: ....

....

1 500 000 N

6 000 000 N

1 500 000 N

1 500 000 N

Think... the resultant force is the force that's <u>left</u> when you take into account all the individual forces.

Q2 Khaleeda helps Jenny investigate **falling objects**. Jenny lets go of a **beach ball** and Khaleeda times how long it takes to fall. Khaleeda draws the distance-time graph — it looks like the one shown.

Which phrase below describes points X, Y and Z?
Explain your answer to each point.

forces in balance **reaction force from ground acts**
unbalanced force of gravity

X: ....

....

Y: ....

....

Z: ....

....

Distance from dropping point (m)

Z

Y

X

Time (s)

Q3 Place the following four **trucks** in order of **increasing momentum**.

Truck A
speed = 30 m/s
mass = 3000 kg

Truck B
speed = 10 m/s
mass = 4500 kg

Truck C
speed = 20 m/s
mass = 4000 kg

Truck D
speed = 15 m/s
mass = 3500 kg

....

....

....

(lowest momentum) .... , ... , ... , ... (highest momentum)

Top Tips: Another thing to remember about momentum (apart from the equation) is that it **changes** when a resultant force acts on an object. So if truck A started to brake, there'd be a resultant backwards force, and the truck's momentum would decrease. More on that coming up next...

Change in Momentum and Force

Q1 A **boat** was travelling through the water in a straight line at constant speed.
A wave hit the side of the boat, exerting a resultant force of **8000 N** for **1.9 seconds**.

a) Calculate the resulting change in the boat's momentum.

....

....

....

b) A few minutes later, the boat was hit by another wave. Its **change** in momentum was roughly the **same** as last time, but the force of the wave acted over a **shorter time**. What does this tell you about the average force acting on the boat during the second wave?

....

....

Q2 Modern cars are equipped with many **safety features** that reduce the **forces** acting on passengers during a collision.

a) Explain how a **crumple zone** reduces the forces acting on passengers during a collision.

Increases time of collision between object & car making it longer so resultant force is less.

b) Give **two other** car safety features that work in a similar way.

1. *Seatbelt*

2. *Airbag.*

Q3 A **1200 kg car** is travelling at **30 m/s** along the motorway.
It crashes into the barrier of the central reservation and is stopped in a period of **1.2 seconds** (after which its momentum is **zero**).

a) Find the momentum of the car **before** the crash.

....

b) Find the size of the **average force** acting on the car as it stops.

....

....

c) Explain why the occupants of the car are likely to be less severely injured if they are wearing seat belts made of slightly **stretchy** material.

....

....

Work

Q1 Circle **one** word in each sentence to make them correct.

a) Work involves the transfer of **force** / **momentum** / **energy**.

b) To do work a **force** / **push** acts over **a distance** / **time**.

c) Work is measured in **watts** / **joules**.

Q2 Tick the boxes to show whether the following statements are **true** or **false**.

	True	False
a) Work is done when a toy car is pushed along the ground.	☑	☐
b) No work is done if a force is applied to an object which does not move.	☑	☐
c) Gravity does work on an apple that is not moving.	☐	☐
d) Gravity does work on an apple that falls out of a tree.	☐	☐

Q3 An elephant exerts a constant force of **1200 N** to push a donkey along a straight flat track at a steady speed of **1 m/s**.

a) Calculate the work done by the elephant if the donkey moves **8 m**.

....

b) What form(s) of energy is the work done on the donkey transferred into?

....

....

Q4 Ben's weight is **600 N**. He climbs a ladder. The rungs of the ladder are **20 cm** apart.

a) What force is Ben doing work **against** as he climbs?

....

b) How much work does Ben do when he climbs **10 rungs**? (Ignore any 'wasted' energy.)

....

....

20 cm

Don't forget to think about the underlined units.

c) How many rungs of the ladder must Ben climb before he has done **15 kJ** of work? (Ignore any 'wasted' energy.)

....

....

Top Tips: Pretty much every 'work done' question you'll come across talks about moving something horizontally. Moving something vertically is exactly the same in principle though — you're just applying a force (at least equivalent to the object's weight) to move the object upwards.

Module P4 — Explaining Motion

Kinetic Energy

Q1 Find the **kinetic energy** of a **200 kg** tiger running at a speed of **9 m/s**.

....

....

Q2 A **golf ball** is hit and given **9 J** of kinetic energy.
The ball's speed is **20 m/s**. What is its **mass**?

....

....

Q3 A **60 kg** skydiver jumps out of an aeroplane and free-falls.
Find the skydiver's **speed** if she has **90 750 J** of kinetic energy.

....

....

Q4 A large truck and a car both have a kinetic energy of **614 400 J**.
The mass of the truck is **12 288 kg** and the car **1200 kg**.

a) Calculate the **speed** of:

i) the car ....

ii) the truck ....

b) John has a remote-controlled toy car and truck. The car's mass is 100 g
and the truck's is 300 g. The car is moving twice as fast as the truck.
Which has more kinetic energy — the car or the truck? Explain your answer.

Think about how doubling speed or trebling mass affects K.E.

....

....

Q5 Jack is riding his **bicycle** along a level road and has a total kinetic energy of **1440 J**.
His dad gives him a push, exerting a force of **200 N** on the bicycle.

a) Explain why the push will **increase** Jack's velocity.

....

....

b) What assumption would you need to make to calculate Jack's increase in velocity? Why?

....

....

Module P4 — Explaining Motion

Gravitational Potential Energy

Q1 Fred works at a DIY shop. He has to load **28 flagstones** onto the delivery truck. Each flagstone weighs **250 N** and has to be lifted **1.2 m** onto the truck.

Use the equation that links G.P.E. weight and height.

a) How much gravitational potential energy does **one** flagstone gain when lifted onto the truck?

....

....

1.2 m

b) What is the **total gravitational potential energy** gained by the flagstones after they are **all** loaded onto the truck?

....

c) How much **work** does Fred do loading the truck?

....

Q2 A **roller coaster** carriage and its passengers are **stationary** at the top of a ride. At this point they have a gravitational potential energy of **300 kJ**. The full carriage has a mass of **750 kg**.

a) Draw lines to connect the correct energy statement with each stage of the carriage's journey.

A

B

C

D

A minimum G.P.E., maximum K.E.

B K.E. is being converted to G.P.E.

C maximum G.P.E.

D G.P.E. is being converted to K.E.

b) i) When the carriage is at **half** its original height, how much **kinetic energy** should it have?

....

ii) Calculate the speed of the carriage at this point.

....

....

iii) Explain why the speed is **less** than this in real life.

....

....

....

Gravitational Potential Energy

Q3   Jo is sitting at the top of a **helter-skelter ride** and her weight is **500 N.**

a) At the top of the helter-skelter, Jo's gravitational potential energy is **4000 J** greater than it was on the ground. How high up is she?

....

b) She comes down the helter-skelter and at the bottom her kinetic energy is **1500 J**. How much **energy** has been 'wasted' coming down the ride?

....

c) Which **force(s)** causes this energy to be wasted?

....

Q4   A skier with a weight of **700 N** rides a chairlift to a point **20 m** higher up a ski slope. She then skis back down to the **same height** as she got on the chairlift.

a) Calculate the **work done** by the chairlift in carrying the skier up the slope.

....

....

b) Assuming no energy is wasted, how much kinetic energy does the skier gain by skiing down the slope?

....

c) The skier has a mass of **70 kg**. What is the maximum **speed** she could reach as she skis down?

....

....

Q5   A toy cricket ball hit straight upwards has a gravitational potential energy of **121 J** at the **top** of its flight.

a) What is the ball's **kinetic energy** just before it hits the ground, assuming no energy is wasted?

....

b) Calculate the **speed** of the ball at this point if its mass is **100 g**.

....

....

Top Tips: Kinetic energy, gravitational potential energy, work done... they're all measured in joules, so they're all energy. If you 'do work' on something, you're converting energy — by exerting a force on the object which makes it move. If you start an object moving or make it speed up you've given it some K.E. If you move the object away from the ground, you've given it some G.P.E.

Module P4 — Explaining Motion

Mixed Questions — Module P4

Q1 Mr Alonso drives his car at a constant speed for **1500 m**. The engine produces a force of **300 N**.

300 N ➡

a) How much work does the engine do?

....

b) Mr Alonso then accelerates, increasing his speed by **20 m/s** over **6.2 s**. Calculate his acceleration.

....

c) Whilst travelling at **20 m/s**, Mr Alonso crashes his car into a tree. The car takes **0.8 s** to stop.
Given that the car has a mass of **1200 kg**, calculate the force acting on the car as it stops.

....

Both momentum equations are needed here.

....

....

d) Explain how Mr Alonso's seat belt reduced the forces acting on him during the crash.

....

....

Q2 Jack and Jill go up a hill to go on a roller coaster. With Jack and Jill in it, the roller coaster carriage has a total mass of **1200 kg** and a weight of **12 000 N**.

a) At the start of the ride the carriage rises up to its highest point of **34 m** above the ground and stops. Calculate its gain in potential energy.

....

b) The carriage then falls to a **third** of its maximum height. Assuming there is no air resistance or friction, calculate the **speed** of the carriage at this point.

....

....

....

c) At the end of the ride, the carriage slows down, decelerating at **6.4 m/s²**.
How long does it take the carriage to slow down from **12 m/s** and come to a stop?

....

....

Module P4 — Explaining Motion

Mixed Questions — Module P4

Q3   Norman loves trainspotting. As a special treat, he not only notes the train numbers but plots a **distance-time** graph for two of the trains.

a)   For how long is train 2 stationary?

....

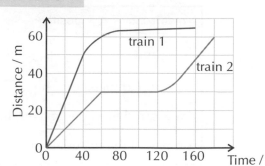

b)   Both trains start at a steady speed.
How do we know this?

....

c)   Calculate the initial speed of the faster train between 0 s and 40 s.

....

d)   Describe the motion of train 1 between 40 s and 80 s.

....

Q4   In the film 'Crouching Sparrow, Hidden Beaver', a dummy weighing **950 N** is dropped **60 m** from the top of a building.

a)   Sketch a distance-time graph and a velocity-time graph for the dummy from the moment it is dropped until it hits the ground.
(Ignore air resistance and assume the dummy has a constant acceleration).

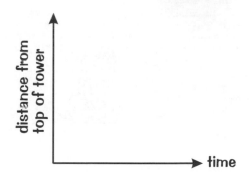 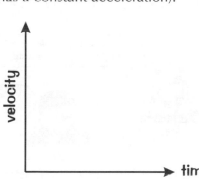 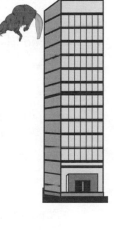

b)   Do any forces act on the dummy when it lies still on the ground (after falling)?
If so, what are they?

....

c)   The take doesn't go to plan so the dummy is lifted back to the top of the building using a motor.

i)   How much work is done on the dummy to get it to the top of the building?

....

ii)   The motor lifts the dummy at a speed of 0.8 m/s.
How long does it take to get the dummy to the top of the building?

....

Static Electricity

Q1 Fill in the gaps in these sentences with the words in the box.

electrons	positive	static	friction	insulating	negative

........*static*........ electricity can build up when two ......*insulating*........... materials

are rubbed together. The ....*friction*........ causes ....*electrons*....... to be

transferred from one material onto the other. This leaves a ....*negative*......... charge

on one of the materials and a ....*positive*........... charge on the other.

Q2 **Circle** the pairs of charges that would **attract** each other and **underline** those that would **repel**.

positive and positive   (positive and negative)   (negative and positive)   negative and negative

Q3 Tick the boxes to show whether the following statements are **true** or **false**.

		True	False
a)	Electrons are negatively charged particles.	✓	
b)	Areas of positive charge are caused by the movement of positive charges.		✓
c)	Negatively charged areas occur because electrons are attracted to each other.		✓

Q4 Three friends are talking about some of the effects of **static electricity**.

Why does my hair sometimes stick out and cling to my hairbrush?

Why is the TV screen always dusty — my mum cleans it all the time?

Why do I hear a crackling sound when I take off my jumper?

Lisa   Tim   Sara

Answer their questions in terms of the **attraction** and **repulsion** between charges.

Lisa: ...... *repulsion* ....

....

Sara: ...... *repulsion* ....

....

Tim: ...... *attraction.* ....

....

Top Tips: Static electricity's responsible for many of life's little irritations — bad hair days, dusty surfaces and those little shocks you get from touching car doors and even stroking the cat.

Electric Current

Q1 Complete the following sentences by choosing the correct words from the box.

| flow | voltage | resistance | charge | ohms | current | force | amperes |

a) Current is the ....*flow*........ of ....*electrons*........ round a circuit.

b) ....*Voltage*........ acts like a ....*force*........ that pushes the current round the circuit.

c) ....*Resistance*........ restricts the flow of current round the circuit.

Q2 Draw a line to connect each quantity with the **name** and **symbol** of its unit.

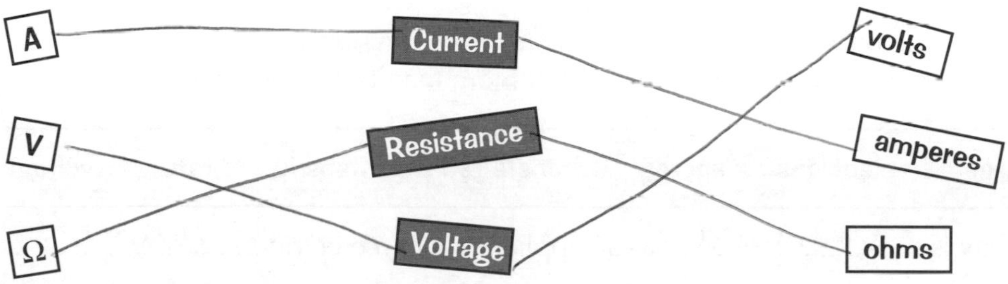

Q3 Tick the boxes to show whether the following statements are **true** or **false**.

		True	False
a)	In a circuit, the charge gets used up.		✓
b)	A component, such as a lamp or motor, resists the flow of charge through it.	✓	
c)	Current can't flow through an insulator because the charges aren't free to move.	✓	
d)	The wires in an electric circuit are full of charges that are fixed in place.		✓

Q4 The **flow** of electricity in circuits can be compared to the flow of water in pipes.

a) "The pipes in a water 'circuit' are full of water that is free to move."
What is the equivalent of this statement for an **electrical circuit**?

........*Battery? the flow*........

........*of charge.*........

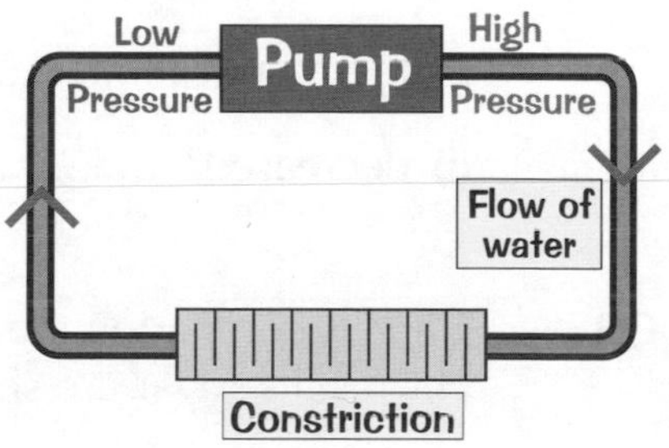

b) What electrical device does the pump
in the water 'circuit' correspond to? ....*Battery.*........

c) The system in the diagram has a constriction where it is harder for the water to flow.
What corresponds to this constriction in an electrical circuit?

........*Resistor.*........

d) The pump is turned up. What would the equivalent action be in an electrical circuit?

........*Increase Voltage.*........

Electric Current

Q5 Ranjit makes the electric circuit shown in the diagram. The lamp lights up, but when Ranjit opens the **switch** it goes out. He discusses why this happens with his friends.

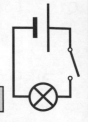

Brian says: "All the charge must have been used up when the switch was closed."

Lara says: "When the switch is open, charge leaks out and so doesn't reach the lamp."

Ranjit says: "The circuit is not complete when the switch is open so no current flows."

Which person has the correct explanation? ....

Q6 Complete the paragraph by choosing words from the box.
You might need to use some of the words more than once, or not at all.

charge electrons energy transferred intensity rate voltage

Energy is ......*transferred*.... to an appliance when electric ......*charge*........

flows through it. The ....*rate*................. at which an appliance transfers

.............*energy*.......... from the charge is the power rating of the appliance.

Q7 The current that flows in a circuit is determined by the sizes of the **forces** pushing it and opposing it.

World's Strongest Current

a) Describe how the voltage of the battery affects the size of the current that will flow.

....

b) Without changing the voltage of the battery, how could the current be:

i) increased? ....*take   away   resistor*..................................

ii) decreased? ....*add   resistor.*...

Q8 Chris is comparing the voltage, current and power of three **CD players**. His results so far are shown in the table below.

Fill in the missing values to complete the table.

You'll need the equation which connects power, current and voltage.

	Player A	Player B	Player C
Voltage (V)	12		230
Current (A)	2.5	40	
Power (W)		120	460

Electric Circuits

Q1   Match up these items from a standard test circuit with the correct **description** and **symbol**.

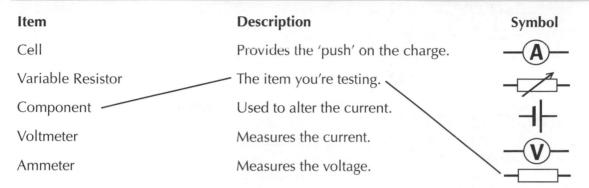

Item	Description	Symbol
Cell	Provides the 'push' on the charge.	
Variable Resistor	The item you're testing.	
Component	Used to alter the current.	
Voltmeter	Measures the current.	
Ammeter	Measures the voltage.	

Q2   The diagram below shows a complete **circuit**.

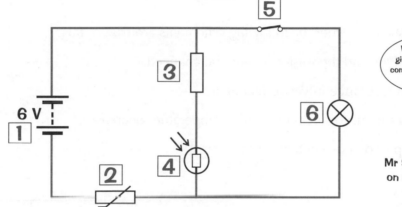

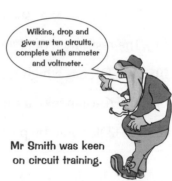

Wilkins, drop and give me ten circuits, complete with ammeter and voltmeter.

Mr Smith was keen on circuit training.

a)   Give the name of each of the numbered components.

1. ....   2. ....   3. ....

4. ....   5. ....   6. ....

b)   Draw an ammeter on the circuit in the correct position to measure the current **leaving the battery**.

c)   Draw a voltmeter on the circuit in the correct position to measure the voltage **across the lamp**.

Q3   Complete the following passage by choosing the correct words from the box.
Each word may be used once, more than once, or not at all.

charge	battery	potential difference	current
parallel	energy	series	components

Voltage (or ....) measures how much ....

is transferred to or from the .... as it moves between two points.

The .... transfers .... to the charge

and .... transfer it away from the charge. A voltmeter must be

connected in ....

Resistance

Q1 The graph below shows V-I curves for four resistors: A, B, C and D.

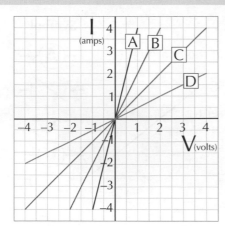

$$\text{Resistance} = \frac{\text{voltage}}{\text{current}}$$

a) Which resistor has the highest resistance? ....

b) Explain your answer to part **a)**.

....

c) Calculate the resistance of resistor B.

....

Q2 Tick the boxes to show whether the following statements are **true** or **false**.

		True	False
a)	The resistance of LDRs and thermistors cannot be changed.	☐	☐
b)	An LDR has a high resistance in very bright light.	☐	☐
c)	The resistance of a thermistor increases as the temperature decreases.	☐	☐
d)	An LDR could be part of a useful thermostat.	☐	☐

Q3 Fill in the missing values in the table on the right.

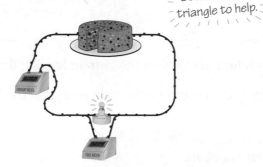

Use a formula triangle to help.

Voltage (V)	Current (A)	Resistance (Ω)
6	2	
8		2
	3	3
4	8	
2		4
	0.5	2

Q4 Leyla was doing her homework when the light on her desk went out. Leyla's mum said the bulb had blown and needed replacing, but that they should wait until it had cooled before touching it.

a) What causes the filament in the lamp to get hot when current passes through it?

....

....

b) Why are the filaments in lamps designed to have a very high resistance?

....

Resistance

Q5 Peter's teacher has given him an unlabelled resistor. Peter plans an experiment to work out its resistance but he is worried that the resistance of the **wires** in his test circuit will affect his results.

a) i) What is normally assumed about the resistance of the wires in a circuit?

....

ii) Why would this assumption be unlikely to make Peter's results inaccurate?

....

b) Peter plans to vary the current through the resistor and take several pairs of voltage-current readings. Explain how he could work out the resistance from these readings.

....

....

Q6 Miriam is testing three components (A, B and C) using a standard test circuit. She knows that component A is a **fixed resistor**, but doesn't know what components B and C are.

a) Sketch a graph on the axes on the right to show how the current through **component A** would vary with voltage.

Component A

b) While Miriam was testing **component B**, her friend Lakisha opened the blinds covering the windows. The graph below shows Miriam's results. Lakisha opened the blinds at the point marked 'X' on the graph.

Component B

i) What effect did opening the blinds have on the **resistance** of component B?

....

....

ii) What might component B be? ....

c) **Component C** is used as part of a thermostat and its resistance changes with **temperature**.

i) What is component C? ....

ii) Describe how the resistance of component C will change as it is gradually warmed.

....

....

Top Tips: There are two very important skills you need to master for resistance questions — interpreting V-I graphs and using the formula $R = V \div I$. Make sure you can do both.

Series Circuits

Q1 Draw lines to match up these descriptions with what they describe in a **series circuit**.

Same everywhere in the circuit

Shared by all the components

The sum of the resistances

Can be different for each component

Potential difference

Current

Total potential difference

Total resistance

Q2 The diagram shows a series circuit.

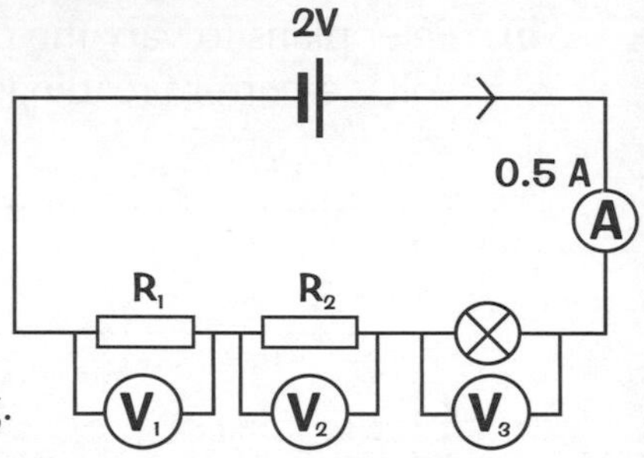

a) What component could be added to the circuit to **increase** the total voltage?

....

b) Voltmeter V_1 has the lowest reading and V_3 has the highest reading.

i) Which component has the highest **resistance**? ....

ii) What does this tell you about the amount of work done by the charge passing through each component?

....

c) Why is the **total resistance** of the circuit greater than the resistance of any one of the components?

....

Q3 Vikram does an experiment with different numbers of lamps in two series circuits. The diagram on the right shows his two circuits.

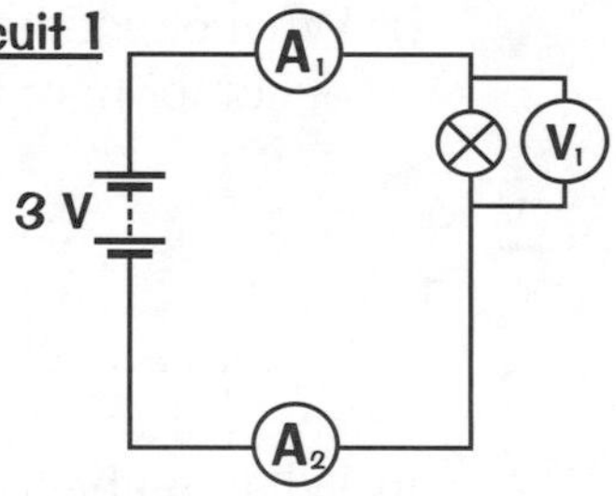

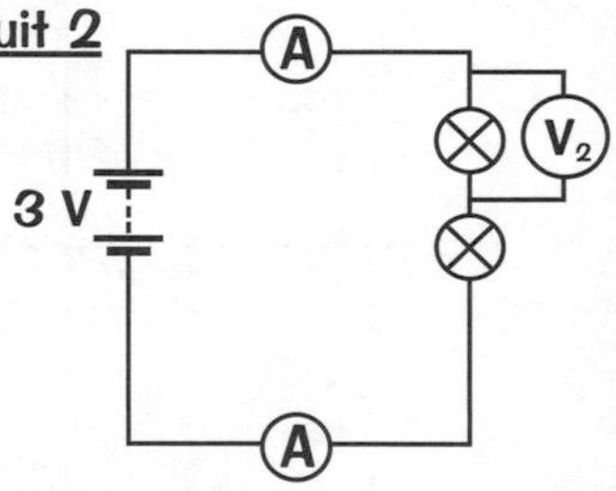

a) The reading on ammeter A_1 in circuit 1 is **0.2 A**.

i) What is the reading on ammeter A_2? ....

ii) How do you know this? ....

b) Vikram is puzzled because the two voltmeters show different readings, even though all the lamps are the same.

i) Which voltmeter shows the **higher** reading? ....

ii) Explain, in terms of work done, why the voltage across the lamps is different for each circuit.

....

....

....

Parallel Circuits

Q1   Tick to show whether these statements about parallel circuits are **true** or **false**.

True   False

a)   Components are connected separately to the power supply.   ☐   ☐

b)   Each component has the same potential difference across it.   ☐   ☐

c)   Components can be switched on and off independently.   ☐   ☐

Q2   Karen does an experiment with different numbers of identical lamps in three parallel circuits. The diagrams on the right show her three circuits.

Explain what happens to the following quantities when more lamps are added in parallel:

a)   The voltage across each lamp. ....

....

b)   The current passing through each lamp. ....

....

c)   The resistance of each lamp. ....

....

Q3   The diagram opposite shows a parallel circuit. Ammeter A_2 has a reading of **0.27 A** and A_3 has a reading of **0.43 A**.

a)   i)   What reading is shown on ammeter A_1? ....

ii)   Explain your answer. ....

....

b)   i)   Which resistor has the **smallest** resistance? Explain your answer.

....

....

ii)   Will the **total** resistance be larger, smaller or equal to the resistance of this resistor? Why?

....

....

c)   The branch containing resistor R_2 is removed from the circuit.
What is the new reading on ammeter A_2?

....

Mains Electricity

Q1 The National Grid distributes **mains electricity** around the UK.

a) At what voltage is mains electricity supplied to people's homes?

....

b) What is the difference between the current supplied by a battery and mains electricity?

....

c) What is the name of the process that generators use to produce electricity?

....

Q2 Choose words from the box to fill in the blanks in this paragraph about **generating electricity**.

moving	electromagnetic	magnet	coil	induction
alternating	voltage	reverses	magnetic	complete

You can create a .... across an electrical conductor by

.... a magnet near the conductor. This process is called

.... In simple generators,

a .... is rotated near a .... of wire.

The generator produces a(n) .... current when it is connected

up to a .... circuit.

Q3 Inga is experimenting with a magnet and a coil of wire. When she moves the north pole of the magnet into the coil, a **positive voltage** is induced.

a) In which direction (positive or negative) will the induced voltage be if Inga:

i) Moves the magnet back out of the coil? ....

ii) Pushes the south pole of the magnet into the coil? ....

b) Explain what will happen if Inga:

i) Holds the magnet still inside the coil.

....

ii) Sets up her apparatus so that the magnet moves repeatedly into and out of the coil.

....

Top Tips: There are four factors that can increase the size of an induced voltage — make sure you can list all four of them off by heart. You never know when they might pop up in an exam, or in a practice question like the kind you might find in a book like this... ahem...

Mains Electricity

Q4 A **simple generator** can be made by rotating a magnet inside a coil of wire.

a) When the magnet turns **half a turn**, what happens to the direction of:

i) The magnetic field? ....

ii) The voltage across the coil? ....

b) The magnet is spun in one direction. Does this generate AC or DC in the wire?

....

c) Mains electricity is supplied as alternating current. Explain why this is used.

....

....

Q5 Look at the simple generators sketched below.

A ☐ Coil spread over greater area

B ☐ Quicker rotation

C ☐ More coils

D ☐ Stronger magnet

Tick the box to show which one of the generators labelled A - D will **not** induce a higher voltage than the generator in the box to the left.

Q6 The diagram shows a hamster-powered generator.

a) What happens in the coil of wire when the hamster runs at a constant speed? Explain your answer.

....

....

....

b) What would change if the hamster ran in the opposite direction (at the same speed as before)?

....

c) Suggest **three changes** you could make to the generator to produce a higher voltage.

1. ....

2. ....

3. ....

Transformers

Q1 Number the following statements 1 to 5 in the right order to explain how a **transformer** works.

	This causes a rapidly-changing magnetic field in the core.
	An alternating current can flow in a circuit connected to the secondary coil.
	An alternating current flows in the primary coil.
1	An alternating voltage is connected to the primary coil of a transformer.
	The changing magnetic field induces an alternating voltage in the secondary coil.

Q2 Transformers have a laminated **iron core**.

a) Describe the structure of a transformer.

....

....

b) What is the difference between a step-up and a step-down transformer?

....

....

....

c) Why do transformers work with alternating current only?

....

....

Q3 Use the **transformer equation** to complete the following table.

$$\frac{V_P}{V_S}=\frac{N_P}{N_S} \text{ or } \frac{V_S}{V_P}=\frac{N_S}{N_P}$$

Number of turns on primary coil	Voltage to primary coil (V)	Number of turns on secondary coil	Voltage to secondary coil (V)
1000	12	4000	
1000		2000	20
1000	12		12
	33 000	500	230

Top Tips: Remember that you can use the transformer equation either way up. Handy. It makes it easier to use if you put whichever thing you need to find on the top of the equation.

Magnetic Fields

Q1 The diagram below shows a wire carrying a current passing through a piece of flat card.

a) Some iron filings are sprinkled onto the card. When the current is switched on, a pattern develops in the iron filings because of the magnetic field around the wire.

On the diagram, sketch the pattern that the iron filings make when the current is switched on.

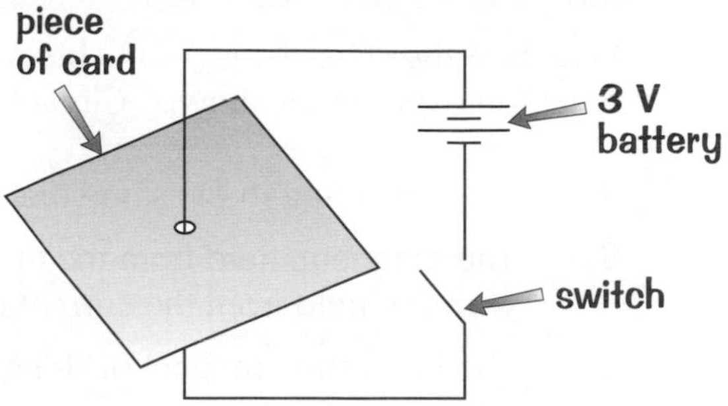

b) The coil of current-carrying wire shown on the right has a stronger magnetic field inside the loop than outside.

Explain why this is, including a sketch of the magnetic field.

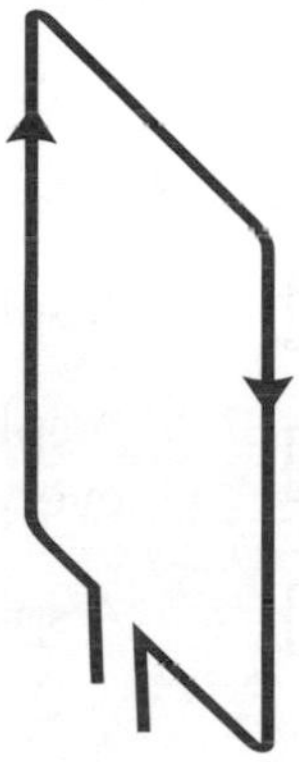

....

....

....

Q2 Tick to show whether the following statements are **true** or **false**. Write a correct version of each false statement.

True False

a) The magnetic field around a current-carrying wire is made up of concentric circles. ☐ ☐

....

b) As more turns are added to a current-carrying coil its magnetic field gets weaker. ☐ ☐

....

c) A current-carrying wire parallel to the lines of force of a magnetic field feels a force. ☐ ☐

....

Q3 The diagram shows an electrical wire between two magnetic poles. When the current is switched on, the wire moves at right angles to the magnetic field.

Use Fleming's LHR.

a) Which way will the wire move?

....

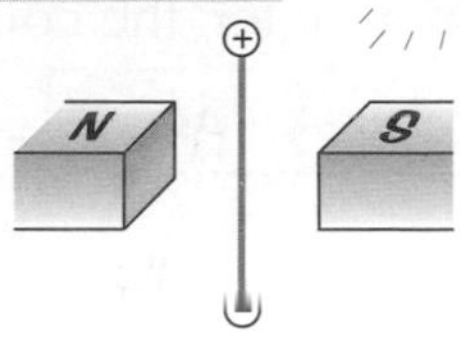

b) Describe one way in which the wire could be made to move in the opposite direction. ....

c) Explain why the wire moves.

....

....

The Motor Effect

Q1 The diagram shows an experiment which illustrates the **motor effect**. When the current is switched on the bar rolls along the rails.

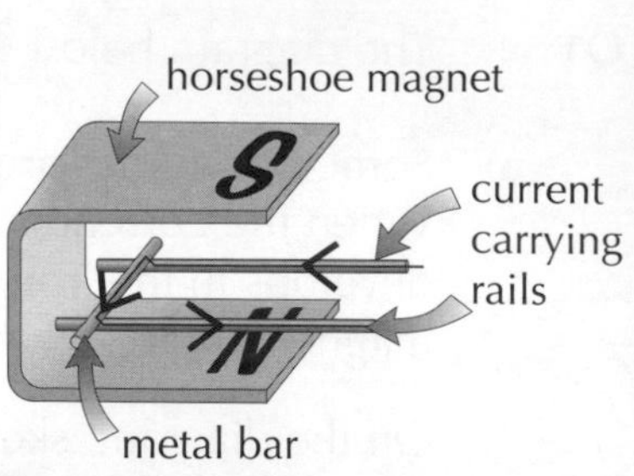

Which of the statements A to D below states correctly what the experiment shows? Circle the appropriate letter.

horseshoe magnet

current carrying rails

metal bar

A   A force acting in the same direction as the current is flowing.

B   The magnetic field from the magnet combining with the field from the current in the bar.

C   The horseshoe magnet pushing the bar along.

D   The current in the bar pulling it along the rails.

Q2 Read the three statements below. Tick the box next to each statement that you think is **true**.

☐   A split-ring commutator makes a motor spin faster.

☑   A split-ring commutator reverses the direction of the current every half turn by swapping the contacts to the DC supply.

☐   A split-ring commutator keeps a motor spinning in the same direction.

Q3 The diagram shows a current-carrying coil in a uniform magnetic field.

north pole   south pole

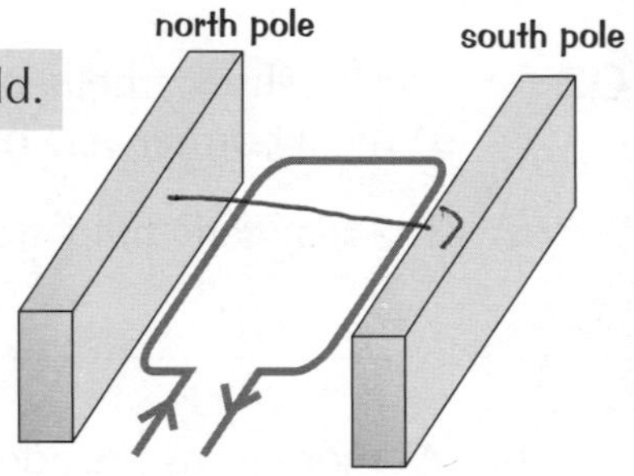

a) Draw an arrow on the diagram to show the direction of the uniform magnetic field.

b) Describe the direction of the force on the **left-hand arm** of the coil.

.... downwards ....

c) In which direction will the coil move — clockwise or anticlockwise? ..... anticlockwise.

d) **i)** This diagram shows the coil just after it has turned through 90°. Draw arrows to show the direction of the forces on each arm of the coil at this stage and describe how you would expect the coil to move.

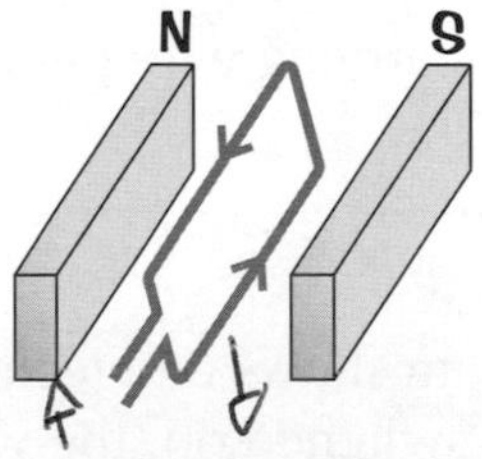

N   S

.... clockwise. ....

ii) In a motor, the coil keeps rotating in the same direction. Explain how this is achieved.

.... At every half-turn, the direction ....
.... of the current is swapped (reversed). ....

e) Describe how the motor effect is used in a DVD player.

Mixed Questions — Module P5

Q1 Paul wants to set the mood for his date with some romantic lighting.
He dims the lights using a dimmer switch which works as a **variable resistor**.

I can still see your face...

a) Describe how the dimmer switch dims the lights.

Think... variable resistors alter current.

....

Position	Resistance (Ω)	Current (A)
1	50	
2		2.3
3		9.2

b) Paul entertains his date by taking some current and resistance readings with the dimmer switch in three different positions. The voltage is 230 V. Complete the table using R = V : I.

c) In which position will the lights be brightest? ....

Q2 Maria walks across the nylon carpet in her living room and touches the radiator to see if it's warm.

a) When she touches the radiator, which is earthed, she feels an electric shock. Explain why.

....

b) The radiator is made of metal, which is a good conductor of electricity.
Explain what makes a material a good electrical conductor.

....

Q3 The diagram shows a circuit in which two resistors and a lamp are connected in **series**.

If the voltmeter shown reads **4 V**, find:

a) the resistance of the lamp. ....

12 V

5 Ω   5 Ω

b) the total resistance of the three components.

....

c) the current flowing in the circuit.

....

d) the power rating of the lamp.

....

Module P5 — Electric Circuits

Mixed Questions — Module P5

Q4 The diagram shows a circuit which could be used for the lights on a car.
Each headlight bulb is rated at **12 V**, **6 A** and each side light bulb is rated at **12 V**, **0.5 A**.

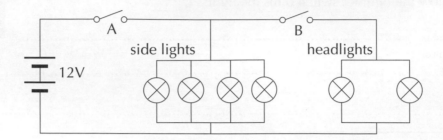

a) Calculate the **total current** flowing from the battery when:

i) Switch A is closed and switch B is open.

....

ii) Switch A is open and switch B is closed.

....

iii) Switches A and B are both closed.

....

b) A car's rear window de-mister is also connected to the battery in parallel.
What will the voltage across the de-mister be? Explain your answer.

....

....

c) The car also has a circuit with a component that can act as a **temperature detector**.

i) Name a component that can be used as a temperature detector.

....

ii) Describe what happens to this component as its temperature **falls**.

....

d) The car is operated by a motor. The diagram below shows a simple motor.
The coil is rotating as shown.

i) Draw arrows labelled 'F' to show the direction
of the force on each arm of the coil.

ii) Draw arrows labelled 'I' on each arm of the coil
to show the direction the current is flowing.

iii) Draw '+' and '–' on the leads of the split-ring commutator
to show the polarity of the power supply.

Radioactivity

Q1 Label this diagram of an atom with the words below.

nucleus   protons   neutrons   electrons

....

(made up of ....

and ....)

....

Q2 **Underline** the correct statement(s) about ionising radiation below.

Ionising radiation can transfer enough energy to break molecules apart.

Unstable atoms can emit three types of ionising radiation.

Theta radiation is a type of ionising radiation.

Q3 Draw **lines** to connect the beginning of each sentence with its ending.

Radioactive atoms are...

Unstable atoms decay...

The decay is spontaneous...

When atoms decay...

...they give out radiation.

...and not affected by physical conditions.

...at random and unpredictably.

...unstable and decay to become stable.

Q4 Chlorine has two stable **isotopes**. Each has 17 protons in its nucleus.

a) What will be different about the nuclei of these two isotopes?

....

b) Define the term isotope.

....

c) What is meant by a **stable isotope**?

Stable is the _opposite_ of unstable.

....

Radiation

Q1 There are **three** types of nuclear radiation.

a) What are these three types?

Alpha, Beta, Gamma

b) Which part of the atom does the radiation come from?

Nucleus

c) Which type of radiation is **not** a particle?

Gamma

DANGER
HARMFUL REVISION
DO NOT READ

Q2 The ability of radiation to **penetrate** a material depends on what kind of radiation it is.

a) Which type(s) of radiation could **escape** from a paper bag?

Beta, Gamma

b) Which type(s) of radiation will **pass through** a thin sheet of aluminium?

Gamma

c) Which type(s) of radiation will be **stopped** by a thin sheet of aluminium?

Beta

Q3 Choose from the words given below to complete the paragraph.
You may have to use a word more than once, or not at all.

electrons   three   big   two   slowly   easily
light   element   heavy   neutrons   penetrate   protons

Alpha particles are relatively .... and ....
and move fairly ......slowly....... . They are stopped .....easily.........
and don't .....penetrate..... far into materials. Alpha particles come from
very ......heavy......... nuclei, and are made of two ......neutrons protons
and ....two........ neutrons. When an atom releases an alpha particle
the atom changes into a different ......element...... because it has two
fewer ......protons...... .

Top Tip: You really need to get to grips with the three kinds of radiation and the differences between them — what they're made of, how far they penetrate and what can stop them.

Radiation

Q4 Uranium-238 decays by giving off an **alpha particle**, as shown by this nuclear equation:

$$^{238}_{92}U \longrightarrow X + ^{4}_{2}He$$

a) Calculate the mass number and proton number of X.

i) The proton number of X is .... ~~234~~ 88

ii) The mass number of X is .... ~~88~~ 234 .

b) Use a periodic table to identify X. ....

Q5 Connect the two parts of these sentences by drawing **lines** between them.

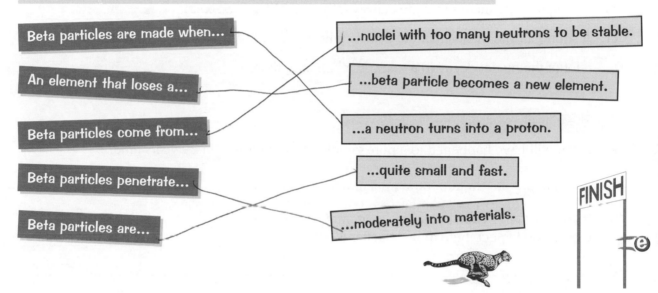

Beta particles are made when...

An element that loses a...

Beta particles come from...

Beta particles penetrate...

Beta particles are...

...nuclei with too many neutrons to be stable.

...beta particle becomes a new element.

...a neutron turns into a proton.

...quite small and fast.

...moderately into materials.

FINISH

Q6 Answer the following questions on gamma radiation.

a) Give **two** ways in which gamma radiation is completely **different** from alpha and beta radiation.

1. .... They don't change atom, they're a wave.

2. .... Aren't easily stopped.

b) In what circumstances would a nucleus emit gamma radiation?

.... When there's too much energy left over

c) Why is a gamma source difficult to store safely?   ⌐ Think about the <u>properties</u> of gamma rays. ¬

.... Very penetrating.

d) Explain why new elements aren't formed when gamma radiation is emitted.

.... only transfer g energy.

....

Half-Life

Q1 Tick the boxes to show whether the following statements are true or false.

True False

a) The number of radioactive nuclei in a sample always stays the same. ☐ ☐

b) Radioactive materials decay at different rates. ☑ ☐

Q2 Complete the following sentences using some of the words given below.

| short | quickly | decay | half | long | melt | slowly | all |

I'm decaying, decaying. What a world, what a cruel, cruel world!

a) The half-life of a sample is the time taken for ...*half*... of the radioactive nuclei present to ...*decay*... .

b) A long half-life means that the activity falls ...*slowly*... .

c) A short half-life means that the activity falls ...*quickly*... because a lot of the nuclei decay in a ...*short*... time.

Q3 The half-life of strontium-90 is **29 years**.

a) What will have happened to a pure sample of strontium-90 in 29 years time?

...*halved.*...

b) If you start with **1000** nuclei of strontium-90, how many would you expect there to be left after **87 years**?

....

Q4 The activity of a radioactive sample is **1440 Bq**. **5 hours** later it has fallen to **45 Bq**. What is the half-life of this material?

It's easiest if you go through the calculation step-by-step.

$\frac{1}{2}$ $\frac{1}{4}$

1440

Q5 The half-life of a radioactive material is **5400 years**.

Bq = becquerel

a) If its activity now is **24 Bq**, how long will it take to drop to **3 Bq**?

....

....

b) How long ago was the sample's activity **96 Bq**?

....

....

Module P6 — Radioactive Materials

The Atom and Nuclear Fusion

Q1   In 1909, **Geiger**, **Marsden** and **Rutherford** conducted an experiment that revolutionised our understanding of the **atom**.

a)   Describe their experiment and results.

....

....

b)   Circle the correct word(s) in each pair to complete this passage.

The nuclear model of the atom describes a **positively** / **negatively** charged region called

the **nucleus** / **neutron** which contains most of the atom's **charge** / **mass**, surrounded by

positively / **negatively** charged electrons. Most of the atom is **empty space** / **matter**.

Q2   Fill in the gaps in the following passage using words from the shaded box.

strong	fusion	mass	positive	light	electrostatic

The charge of a nucleus is always .... In order to fuse,

two nuclei have to overcome the .... force between them

and get close enough for the .... force to hold them together.

Nuclear .... converts .... into energy.

The amount of energy released can be calculated using the equation $E = mc^2$,

where c is the speed of .... in a vacuum.

Q3   Rutherford reached several **conclusions** from his famous experiment. Explain why he arrived at each of the following conclusions after examining the results of the experiment.

a)   'Most of an atom's mass must be concentrated at its centre and the rest empty space.'

....

....

b)   'An atom's nucleus must have a positive charge.'

....

....

Q4   Protons in a nucleus are held together by the **strong nuclear force**. Describe how this force would change as a proton is **moved away** from the other particles in the nucleus.

....

....

Nuclear Fission and Nuclear Power

Q1 Complete the following passage using appropriate words from the grey box.
You may need to use some of the words more than once.

electrons	split	uranium	fission
neutrons	kerosene	equal	protons	nuclei

A nuclear fuel such as ..... _uranium_ .... releases large amounts of energy when

its nuclei ...._split_............ . In nuclear ...._fission_........., neutrons are

fired at the ...._nuclei_..........., causing some of its ....'................... to

split into two smaller nuclei, roughly ...._equal_............... in size. The split also

releases two or three more ...._neutrons_........... .

Q2 Tick the boxes to show which of these statements are **true** and which are **false**.   **True   False**

a) In a nuclear power station the uranium is contained in fuel rods.   ☑ ☐

b) 1 g of uranium releases 10 000 times more energy than 1 g of oil being burnt.   ☑ ☐

c) Nuclear reactions release a similar amount of energy to chemical reactions.   ☐ ☑

d) You can calculate the energy released by nuclear fission using $E = mc^2$.   ☑ ☑

e) Intermediate-level radioactive waste can be buried in secure landfill sites.   ☑ ☐

f) Low-level radioactive waste is sealed in glass and steel and buried underground.   ☐ ☑

Q3 Draw lines to match up the two halves of these statements.

Control rods are used to...   ...are used to carry away the heat.

Coolants such as water and CO_2...   ...nucleus releasing more neutrons.

In nuclear reactors...   ...controlled to prevent overheating.

A neutron splits a uranium...   ...to split more nuclei, releasing more neutrons.

The neutrons released go on...   ...absorb some neutrons.

The chain reaction has to be...   ...a chain reaction is set up.

Nuclear Fission and Nuclear Power

Q4 Nuclear power stations produce **radioactive waste** that is difficult to dispose of. Some people believe this makes nuclear power an unsustainable technology. Circle the **correct word** in each of the following sentences.

a) Clothing that has been used by nuclear technicians is an example of **low** / intermediate / high level waste.

b) A lot of heat is generated by low / intermediate / **high** level waste.

c) The casing of fuel rods is an example of low / **intermediate** / high level waste.

d) Low / **Intermediate** / High level waste is sealed into concrete blocks and put into steel cans.

e) Low / Intermediate / **High** level waste is sealed into glass and steel, and allowed to cool for 50 years before permanent storage.

f) **Low** / Intermediate / High level waste is buried in secure landfill sites.

Q5 Storing radioactive waste is one of the biggest problems that the nuclear industry has. The most likely solution will be underground storage.

a) The site chosen has to be **geologically stable**. What does this mean and why is it important?

No earthquakes or could lead to radiation leak.

b) Suggest a reason why even geologically stable sites are often unlikely to be used for storage.

People living around refuse.

c) Where is most intermediate and high level nuclear waste currently stored?

on-site.

d) The rules about storage of radioactive waste are very strict. Why might they **change** in the future?

e) Why is the storage of radioactive waste a problem that will be with us for a very long time?

Top Tips: Nuclear fuel can provide **millions** of times more energy than the same mass of fossil fuel. Given the current concerns about CO_2 emissions from burning fossil fuels, you can see why many people see nuclear fuel as an attractive alternative. Nuclear waste is really **dangerous** though.

Module P6 — Radioactive Materials

Danger from Radiation

Q1 Complete the paragraph below using the words in the box.

| cells | cancer | ions | sickness | kill | break | ionising |

Alpha, beta and gamma radiation can be described as .... radiation

because when they hit molecules they can .... them into bits

called .... A high dose of radiation will ....

cells causing radiation ...., whereas smaller doses damage cells,

which can cause ....

Q2 We can be affected by ionising radiation in two ways — **contamination** and **irradiation**.

a) Explain the difference between contamination and irradiation.

....

....

....

b) Give **one** example of a situation where someone could be:

i) contaminated.

....

ii) irradiated.

....

Q3 The amount of radiation people receive can vary depending on their **profession**.

a) Name **three** groups of people who are at a higher
than average risk from radiation because of their job.

1. ....

2. ....

3. ....

b) For **each** of the **three** groups named in **a)**, explain **where** the extra radiation comes from.

1. ....

2. ....

3. ....

Module P6 — Radioactive Materials

Danger from Radiation

Q4 Explain why ionising radiation can damage parts of the body that aren't **directly** irradiated.

....

....

Q5 **Radiation doses** are measured in Sieverts (Sv).

a) While you are reading this you are receiving about 2 mSv/year. What is causing this?

....

b) The table below shows some typical radiation doses.

	Dose in Sv
Dose required to sterilise medical products	25 000 (single dose)
Typical total radiotherapy dose to cancer tumour	60
50% survival probability, whole body dose	4 (single dose)
Legal worker dose limit (whole body)	0.02 per year
Average dose from all sources in Cornwall	0.008 per year
Average dose from natural radiation	0.002 per year
Typical chest X-ray dose	0.00002 (single dose)
Average dose from a UK to Spain flight	0.00001 (single dose)

i) Explain why most people are happy to have an X-ray taken, even though it means they're exposed to some extra radiation. Use data from the table to explain your answer.

....

....

ii) How many flights from the UK to Spain would the average person need to take in one year to reach **double** the natural radiation dose?

....

iii) A pilot flies from the UK to Spain **and back** 500 times per year.
If he lives in Cornwall, is his annual dose below the legal worker limit?

....

....

Top Tips: Everyone's exposed to a low level of background radiation every day, and you can't do anything about it (unless you fancy wearing a lead-lined suit and breathing apparatus all day long).

Using Ionising Radiation

Q1 Match up the beginnings and endings of the sentences below.

> Background radiation is...

> Naturally radioactive materials...

> Cosmic rays...

> ...come mainly from the Sun.

> ...radiation that is all around us.

> ...include soil, rocks and the air.

Q2 For a radioactive material to be considered '**safe**', its activity should be **at or below** the normal background level.

A sample of cobalt-60 has an activity of 24 Bq. The background count is 6 Bq. The half-life of cobalt-60 is 5 years. How long will it take for the sample to reach a 'safe' level of activity?

....

Q3 Gamma rays can damage cells and cause cancer. They are also used to **treat** cancer by radiotherapy. A **narrow beam** of gamma rays is focused onto the cancer cells and kills them.

a) Explain why it's important in radiotherapy to use a narrow beam of gamma rays and to focus it carefully.

....

b) Why do patients often feel very ill after radiotherapy?

....

Q4 Surgical instruments used to be made of metal and were **sterilised** by boiling. Now many are made of plastic and are sterilized by gamma rays.

a) The gamma source used to irradiate instruments normally has a long half-life. Why is this?

....

b) Name something else that gamma rays are often used to sterilise. ....

Q5 The table shows the properties of **four** radioisotopes.

Which radioisotope would be best to use as a medical tracer and why?

....

....

Radioisotope	Half-life	Type of emission
technetium-99m	6 hours	gamma
phosphorus-32	14 days	beta
cobalt-60	5 years	beta/gamma
radium-226	1600 years	alpha

....

....

Module P6 — Radioactive Materials

Mixed Questions — Module P6

Q1 Beta emitters are often used as radioactive **tracers** in medicine.

a) Explain what is meant by the word 'tracer'.

....

....

b) Give two reasons why an alpha source would not be suitable to use as a medical tracer.

1. ....

2. ....

c) Complete the nuclear equation for the decay of iodine-131 by beta emission.

$$^{131}_{53}I \rightarrow \; ^{.....}_{.....}Xe + \; ^{0}_{-1}e$$

Q2 The diagram below shows a uranium nucleus **splitting**, which releases energy.

a) What is the name of the process shown in the diagram? ....

b) This process forms part of a chain reaction. Describe what happens in this chain reaction.

....

....

....

c) Nuclear fusion also releases energy. Briefly describe what happens in a nuclear fusion reaction.

....

....

Q3 We are exposed to **background** radiation all the time.
Some of this background radiation comes from radioactive **waste**.

a) Name one other source of background radiation. ....

b) Draw lines to connect each level of radioactive waste with the correct disposal method.

Low-level waste

High-level waste

Intermediate-level waste

Sealed in concrete blocks and steel canisters.

Buried in secure landfill sites.

Sealed in glass and steel then left to cool.

<u>Mixed Questions — Module P6</u>

Q4   Fay measures the **activity** of a sample of copper-64. The graph below shows her results.

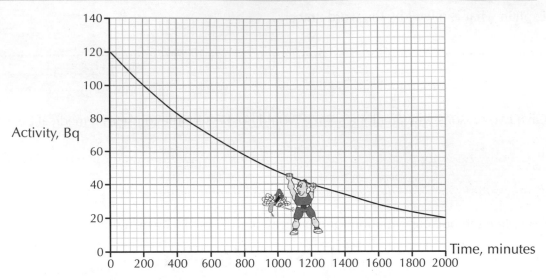

a)   Find the half-life of copper-64. Give your answer in hours.

....

b)   Copper-64 emits beta and gamma radiation. **Circle** a material that will block beta radiation and **underline** a different material that will block gamma radiation:

> **thick lead**   **paper**   **thin aluminium**

c)   Copper-64 emits ionising radiation. What effects can ionising radiation have on living cells?

....

....

Q5   One use of radiation is **radioactive dating**. Approximately one in 10 000 000 of the carbon molecules found in living plants or animals are atoms of the radioactive isotope **carbon-14**. After a plant or animal dies this proportion decreases. Carbon-14 has a half-life of 5730 years.

a)   How **old** is a bone fragment in which the proportion of carbon-14 is one part in 40 000 000?

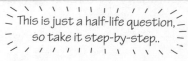
This is just a half-life question, so take it step-by-step..

....

....

....

b)   Carbon-14 is an isotope of carbon. What does the term isotope mean?

....

....

c)   Name another, non-medical, use of radiation. ....